Here's What People Are Saying About The Inspiration Book Series...

A Collegiate EmPowerment Book Series

Stories of Encouragement, EmPowerment & Motivation For College Students

What people are saying about *Inspiration for RAs:*

"Powerful stories from people closest to the action. A must-read for RAs, professional housing staff and all who appreciated the contribution RAs make each day to resident students. Great Job!"
Gary Schwarzmueller, former Executive Director of ACUHO-I

"The RA position is as fun as it is challenging. This book offers an encouraging inspirational message that will keep any RA motivated to make a difference."
Joe Patane, From MTV's Real World Miami and Former RA at UC Berkley

What people are saying about *Inspiration for Student Leaders:*

"This book is not only an inspiration, but a collection of thought provoking writings that will enrich and challenge every student."
Chuck Simpson, Associate Director of Campus Activities at the SUNY Upstate Medical University

"No matter whether you're a student or a professional this is just what the doctor ordered to reenergize the spirit of any leader."
Larry Mannolini, Director of Student Programs & Leadership Development at Lycoming College

What people are saying about *Inspiration for Greeks:*

"This book will touch and nurture the soul of any Fraternity Man or Sorority Woman who reads it."
Mark Victor Hansen, Creator of The #1 New York Times Bestselling Chicken Soup For The Soul® Book Series

"Fraternity and sorority life is a wonderful life-long commitment. It can be full of fun, challenges, learning and inspiration. This book offers an insight into some of these experiences."
Melissa T. Flanagan, Past President of The Association of Fraternity Advisors

What people are saying about *Inspiration for LGBT Students:*

"Inspiration for LGBT Students & Their Allies fulfills its promise. From poetry to personal essay to verse that defies definition, each entry offers hope and a sense of community. Readers are bound to find a piece of themselves in this book."
Jennifer Smith-Holladay, Director of Tolerance.org
A Project of The Southern Poverty Law Center

"No matter how many barriers we overcome, how many firsts we enjoy, how many opportunities we demand access to, we must never forget the fear and shame that many young people feel as they struggle with their own sexual orientation. It's hard, and it's scary, and it's life shaping. We have a responsibility to demonstrate to them that a joyous, rewarding, achievement filled life can be theirs. If this book boosts the self-esteem of one young gay man or woman, or if one friend chooses an embrace over awkwardness, then this book has served its purpose."
T.J. Sullivan, Managing Partner, CAMPUSPEAK, Inc.

Inspirati!n ™

for Student Programmers

Encouragement, Humor & Motivation For Student Programmers

The Collegiate EmPowerment® Press

Collegiate EmPowerment
Helping You Take Higher Education Deeper ™
Easton, Pennsylvania • Princeton, New Jersey
Toll Free: 1-877-EDUTAIN (338-8246)

www.Collegiate-EmPowerment.org

Co-Authored By:
Duane Brown, Ed Cabellon, Jack Gottlieb, Kristen Hyman, Bethany Lombard, Holly Nonnemacher and Joe Urbanski

Published By:
The Collegiate EmPowerment Press

A Funky Little Imprint of:
Collegiate EmPowerment

Helping You Take Higher Education Deeper[TM]
Easton, Pennsylvania o Princeton, New Jersey
Toll Free: 1-877-EDUTAIN (338-8246)
www.Collegiate-EmPowerment.org

Printed with Pride in The United States Of America.
ISBN: 978-0-9646957-5-7

Books are available in quantity discounts when used for student
development and recognition.

We would like to thank all of the contributing authors for
permission to reprint their submissions. Please refer to the back of
this book from individual acknowledgements and copyright use.

This book is dedicated to YOU,
The Student Programmer.
It is YOU who help students
Get An Education, Not Just A Degree.

Table of Contents

In the spirit of Taking Higher Education Deeper,
Collegiate EmPowerment proudly recognizes
The National Association for Campus Activities
As the Charitable Benefactor of
Inspiration for Student Programmers.

Collegiate EmPowerment will donate
One Dollar from every book sold to
The National Association for Campus Activities (NACA).

The NACA Mission Statement:
NACA advances campus activities in higher education
through a business and learning partnership, creating
educational and business opportunities for its school and
professional members.
www.NACA.org

Dear Student Programmer/Advisor,

Thank you for reading *Inspiration for Student Programmers*. The book you are holding has been made possible by people just like you. This book, as well as the entire Inspiration Book Series, is a compilation of stories of encouragement, humor and motivation by college students for college students. Simply put, this book is by YOU and for YOU.

This whole "Inspiration Revolution" was sparked by myself and two college students, Dan Oltersdorf and Amy Connolly-Weber, way back in 1999 when we first published *Inspiration for Resident Assistants*. This book, *Inspiration for Student Programmers* is book number five in the ever expanding series.

What I love most about the Inspiration Series is how it evolves and grows organically- kinda like student programming. It takes something special to create a program or event that works. Some call it magic, while others call it luck. I like to call it Inspiration!

And that is exactly how this book was created. It took one person to inspire us to get the ball rolling with our next book in the Inspiration Book Series. The one person who inspired me to act was one of our co-authors, Holly Nonnemacher. Holly is the Director of Student Activities at Moravian College in the quaint and lovely city of Bethlehem, Pennsylvania.

In the Spring of 2006, Holly and I were having one of our annual lunch meetings at the Bethlehem Brew Works when I asked her the question, "So Holly, what do you think about The Inspiration Book Series?" Holly had used *Inspiration for Student Leaders* to help develop her programming board since its release in 2002.

"Well Tony, I think it is great. I mean we love using *Inspiration for Student Leaders*. But to be honest with you I think the series is missing something." Holly stated.

"What's missing?" I asked.

"A book just for Student Programmers. Don't get me wrong, the other books are great tools, but I think it would be really cool to have a book which truly connects and relates to the unique challenges and opportunities that come with being a student programmer." Holly pressed.

"You are right!" I said. "Let's make it happen!"

And so here, a year and a half later, you now hold in your hands something which was just a vision in another student programmer's mind. It's great to see Inspiration in action. Pretty cool, wouldn't you agree?

The word inspiration literally means- IN SPIRIT. In other words, each and every Inspiration Book has a spirit in it which connects its' own message to its' own type of reader. It is our sincere hope and desire that *Inspiration for Student Programmers* will connect with your spirit too. On behalf of myself and the entire Inspiration for Student Programmer Co-Author Team, thank you for reading this book.

To your continued success!

Anthony J. D'Angelo
Creator of The Inspiration Book Series™

About The Co Authors

Duane Brown is an educational and graphic designer focusing  primarily on the higher education and non-profit sectors. He has worked professionally in higher education in Student Activities, Leadership Development, Student Life, Career Services, and Residence Life. He earned his Bachelor's degree from James Madison University and his Master's degree from Northern Arizona University. When not designing or working with students he can usually be found in a record shop, on a snowboard or road cycling. He performs sketch and improv comedy, and lives in Denver, Colorado.

Ed Cabellon, is a Higher Education professional with over ten  years of progressive Student Affairs experiences including Residential Life, Greek Life, Student Unions/Campus Centers, Orientation, Commuter Services, Student Activities and Leadership Development. Ed has worked at the University of New Hampshire, Central Connecticut State University, Tufts University, and currently works at Bridgewater State College as the Associate Director of the Rondileau Campus Center. He earned his Bachelor of Arts in Communication from Stonehill College and his Masters of Science in Educational Leadership from Central Connecticut State University.

Ed and his wife Becky live in Brockton, MA with their daughters Emilia and Elliana. Ed enjoys spending time with his family and friends; is an avid golfer and basketball player; is a huge Boston sports fan; and owns a small leadership consulting company, LTE Consulting.

Jack Gottlieb is the Executive Director of Campus Impact  Initiatives for Collegiate EmPowerment. His prime focus is to drive a deeper level of lasting results and growth for the student leaders, the groups they are members of and the campus as a whole. Jack is a graduate of Kutztown University in Pennsylvania where he was President of The Association of Campus Events and involved in many other programming roles in other organizations. He is happily married to his wife Jennifer and enjoys playing guitar and going to the gym.

Kristen Hyman currently serves as the Associate Dean and  Director of Student Activities at Villa Julie College in Owings Mills, Maryland. She has worked professionally in higher education in the areas of student involvement, programming, student government, leadership development, and orientation. She holds a Masters in Counseling/College Student Personnel Services from Shippensburg University and a bachelor's degree from the University of Tennessee. She has presented at the national and regional level, written for NACA's Programming magazine, and serves as a Lead Facilitator for the

LeaderShape Institute. Kristen is in her ninth year of professional involvement with NACA and received an Outstanding Service Citation from the Association in 2004 and was named Outstanding New Campus Activities Professional Award by the East Coast region in 2000.

Bethany Lombard is the Managing Editor of the Inspiration Book

Series and the Collegiate EmPowerment Coordinator for Collegiate EmPowerment. Bethany received her Bachelor's degree in Management from Babson College and her Master of Arts in College and University Administration from Michigan State University. Prior to joining the Collegiate EmPowerment Team, Bethany worked on various campuses in Student Activities, Residence Life, Judicial Affairs, and Admissions.

Holly Nonnemacher is currently the Director of Student Activities

at Moravian College in Bethlehem, PA. Holly received both her Bachelor's and Master's degrees from The Pennsylvania State University. She has been a volunteer with the National Association for Campus Activities since 2004 in a variety of regional positions. When not on campus working with students, Holly enjoys spending time with her husband, Nick and their puppy, Peanut.

Joe Urbanski is a Collegiate EmPowerment Coach and The

 Executive Director of Student Seminars. Early on, he learned that his greatest frustration is that most students do not graduate with a sense of meaning and a work of passion. For nearly a decade, Joe has focused his studies on solving this problem, and with the support of his team, he has re-engineered The Orientation To Graduation Seminar Series to reflect this research. Using his Core Genius of creativity, combined with his Core Passion for personal development, Joe is uniquely qualified to guide his audiences in living on purpose.

ACKNOWLEDGEMENTS & APPRECIATION

This project would not be possible without the support, guidance and inspiration of the following individuals. We are very grateful.

Collegiate EmPowerment would like to thank:
All of our clients & students of present, past and future.
Dan Oltersdorf & Amy Connelly for creating the spark.
Holly Nonnemacher for the Inspiration to publish this book.
Our incredible and dedicated co-author team, especially:
Duane Brown for his Core Genius of Design & Packaging.
Bethany Lombard for her Core Genius of Project Management.

Special thanks to John Ogle, Erin Wilson & Alan Davis of NACA for your support and belief in this very worthwhile project.

Duane would like to thank: Mom, Dad, & Craig for everything, my wonderful friends, all my students, Collegiate EmPowerment, Tony D'Angelo for all the inspiration, and Dr. Richard Hill for showing me what true leadership really looks like.

Ed would like to thank: Tony D'Angelo for the opportunity to be part of this amazing project. He continues to be a mentor and inspiration for me. Thanks also to the many Higher Education folks I've met since 1997. You are the reason I do what I do.

Jack would like to thank: Mom and Jennifer for all their love and support.

Kristen would like to thank: Love and gratitude to those who have shared in my growth as a person and a professional: The Fam; hubby Jeff; mentors Mark, Michele, Jan A, Jeff E; BFFs Dawn, Christa.

Bethany would to thank: Tony D'Angelo for believing in me and trusting me with this project. To Mom, Dad, and Derek for all being a part of seeing this book to completion. You all mean the world to me.

Holly would like to thank: My mom and dad for all of the support they have given me over the years. And my husband, Nick, for being there for me day after day!

Joe would like to thank: This thank you is for all student leaders: it is because of you that I am who I am. Thank you for deciding to lead.

Most of all we want to thank each of you
who sent a submission for this project.
Without you this book would not be.
Thank you.

GET AN EDUCATION

not just a degree.

-Anthony J. D'Angelo

An Advisor's Wish for You
By Christa Sandelier

Dear Student Programmer,

When you began your career at this institution you probably planned on meeting some good friends, going to class, getting a degree and maybe becoming involved in an activity or two along the way. You probably entered college with some excitement and nervousness for what was to come. You soon found a few people with whom you shared similar interests and began your new chapter in life. You probably didn't have a clue of what was really to come.

Soon you were consumed with meetings, discussions, reading meeting minutes, talking about bylaws and constitutions – and you probably aren't even a government major, attending workshops, going to diversity training and much more. This was all done in conjunction with attending classes, going to study groups, writing papers, taking exams and attending to the rest of your life. Yes, I said it, you should have a "rest of your life"…you know: exercise, eating, time with friends, maybe attending a spiritual or religious service, working (if you have a job on top of all of this other stuff) and SLEEP!

Well if any of this seems familiar then you deserve the wish I have for you.

I wish that you: hold an officer position and contribute to the betterment of the campus community; get to host a really cool speaker on campus and work your tail off to get it all done; get to stay up all night working on publicity for the big event (just don't make a habit of it); are able to be an advocate for others; are an advocate for yourself; hold true to your values, once you really figure out what those values are; get a great opportunity on a wonderful career as a result of all the hard work you have done; get good grades and remember that if it's not an "A" it might still be a good grade; enjoy what you do; enjoy the people around you; get off campus once and awhile and do something fun in the town/city; find out about the campus history and quirky stories of the past; get to met an alum who shares their campus stories with you; have a fantastic advisor who inspires you to be the best and will challenge you when you are not doing the best; and most of all do what you love to do with passion and enthusiasm!

Give yourself a pat on the back for doing an outstanding job and apply what you have learned from your groups, committees and projects to the rest of your life. When you get out of college and find a job, get involved in your community – life offers a vast array of opportunities.

Sincerely,
Your Advisor

What I Thought About My Programming Board Advisor During...

By Anthony J. D'Angelo

Freshman Summer Orientation:
"Boy that woman looks kinda' young to be a college administrator. I wonder what she does here."

Welcome Back Week:
"Oh, I get it! She is responsible for making all the fun stuff here on campus happen. That's cool."

The Student Organization Fair:
"I met the "fun stuff" lady today. Her name is Jackie. She told me that she is the Director of Campus Activities and serves as the advisor to the programming board. It looks like they do a ton of cool stuff! Fun things like wax hands and sumo wrestling, to leadership conferences and awesome bands and comedians. She actually invited me to see an illusionist who is coming to campus next month for Family Weekend. I can bring my little cousin."

After Family Weekend:
"Wow! Jackie what a cool weekend! My little cousin loved all the stuff we did. That comedian Eric O'Shea made me pee my pants! That guitar guy Dave Binder sounded just like James Taylor and that illusionist- Mike Super- was simply AMAZING. By the way- I saw students with Student Program Board (SPB) shirts helping out all weekend. I didn't realize students play such a key role in making things happen here too. I might join SPB next semester. I will give it some thought over break."

Inspiration for Student Programmers

January of My Freshman Year:
"Hey Jackie! It's great to see you again now that I'm back from break. I have been thinking about programming board. I am ready to join!"

Spring of My Freshman Year:
"Wow, the SPB really does a lot of events here on campus."

Fall of My Sophomore Year:
"Wow, WE really do, do a lot of events here on campus."

Spring of My Sophomore Year:
"I hate my major! I get so much more out of SPB than I do in the classroom. Maybe I should change from biology to marketing/ communications. This way I can apply what I learn in class to what we are actually doing in SPB."

Summer of My Sophomore Year:
"Oh, Hi Jackie! I didn't know that you work during the summer too. I thought you got your summers off, just like the faculty. I'm here picking up some extra classes because I changed my major. I am so much happier now that I am studying what I can apply right away. Thanks for giving me the guidance. You really care about me."

Fall of My Junior Year:
"Jackie, it's past midnight. What are you still doing here on campus? Don't you have to be at the 8am Dean's meeting tomorrow morning? WOW! You work really, really hard. Thanks for all that you do."

Spring of My Junior Year:
"Really Jackie? You think I should run for president of SPB! Thanks for your belief in me."

Fall of My Senior Year:
"It's my senior year Jackie! I know we got a ton of events lined up but one of the most important things you've taught me over the years is to make my successor better than me. So I better start developing next year's leaders now. Thanks for showing me the way!"

Spring of My Senior Year:
"Jackie, I can't believe it is all coming to an end! This is our last major event- Spring Fling. I look forward to making it the best ever."

Graduation Day:
"You'll never understand how much of an impact you've had on me Jackie. I am forever grateful for all that you have taught me. Thank you!"

Years Later:
"I wonder how Jackie would have handled this. She sure knows a lot. Boy do I miss her."

Endless Opportunities For Networking
By Stephanie Thomas

The networking opportunities available in programming are endless. You can advance your network when talking to performers, agency representatives, with students who later work in the field, colleagues who attend conferences with you and share ideas, and with other offices on campus. Anyone who does not take advantage of the networking possibilities is hindering themselves and their campus community. There is so much to learn just by communicating with others in the field and by getting involved in a network.

Personally, I took the steps to advance my networking capabilities by becoming involved with a regional programming association. It allowed me to get to know colleagues from surrounding states which in turn helped me to block book programs to save my campus money. I was also able to share ideas about how programs and services operate at other smaller campuses.

By taking advantage of networking opportunities you are taking the next step to advancing yourself. When you become involved with volunteer positions to help plan events, you are representing your institution and allowing other schools to see your capabilities which in turn could lead you to career options and advancements in the future. You most likely will not stay in your entry-level higher education programming job for your entire career. You can advance yourself, with less stress in the application and interview process, by looking for a new position or advancing your career through volunteer and networking opportunities that can become a part of your resume. Don't miss the opportunity to network!

For Those Who Doubt
By Holly Nonnemacher

As an undergraduate student, I was involved in our Student Government Association which was the programming organization for our campus. I loved being involved and making a difference for my fellow students. It also gave me incentive to do well in my classes since I had transferred to this university from another because I wasn't doing as well academically as I had hoped.

But by transferring to this university getting involved gave me the incentive to improve my grades. First there was a GPA minimum requirement to be involved, and second I was becoming better acquainted with the university. Now when I needed help, I knew where to get it. I was proud of my accomplishments. But it seemed that not everyone believed my involvement was helping.

During a routine meeting with my academic advisor, she mentioned to me that if I would only stop wasting my time on my outside involvements, I would be an honor student. I was devastated – how could she not see that this was actually helping? I left that meeting feeling lost. Was she right?

Perhaps she was right. But as I thought about it, I realized that, yes, I would stop being involved and stay in my room and study every waking moment, and then I could possibly be an honor student. But would I be happy? Would I be a well rounded student who had experiences that I could draw on to understand the concepts we were learning – probably not?

Inspiration for Student Programmers

So I never was an honor student – but I was a good student who had some of the most amazing experiences that made me who I am. So be prepared that not everyone you encounter will understand what you do as a programmer, and some will even doubt its importance. But stay strong and know that you are building a foundation upon which the knowledge you obtain in class can firmly sit.

The Door
By Ana Maria Tosado-Bernier, M.S.

Central Connecticut State University (CCSU) was supposed to be the solution to all my problems. I had decided to transfer to this school in my home state after a very tumultuous freshman year at a small, Methodist college in Central Florida. I decided to transfer to CCSU so I could start fresh, be closer to my family, and hopefully start on the path to a better life.

But Central wasn't the dream I thought it would be. Here I was an insignificant transfer student who knew no one or nothing on the campus. Days were spent going to class ... and that was pretty much it. I felt so alone and lost. I felt like I was wasting all my days away, just wishing for the life it seemed most of the other students had. I had no clue how to start on a path to actually having a campus life and I started to feel as if moving to CCSU was just as big a mistake as attending my old school in Florida.

One afternoon after classes were done for the day, I wandered into the Student Center in the middle of campus. The old building was buzzing with students, some running through the doors that led to the arcade, others walking through the iron gates of the Devil's Den to buy lunch, some walking through the double black doors to the bookstore and of course, a few heading through the wooden doors that led into the school newspaper and radio station. I didn't follow those students through those doors though ... I was drawn to another door – a door that was perched wide open, as if inviting me in ... as if it had been waiting for me, welcoming me.

The door I walked through led to the Program Council - a student organization that planned all the major events on campus. Movies, trips, open mics, formal dances, and all other types of activities. I walked into the door and came face to face with a group of diverse students, lounging on desks and old couches, all laughing and talking loudly. When I entered the room, no one stopped to stare at me. No one asked why I was there. They just started talking to me, as if I had always belonged. The graduate students in charge of keeping the council in order came out of their offices and didn't ask me 20 questions. They just naturally joined in the conversation we were all having (about of all things … gummy bears!) and started telling me about all the help I could be as part of the council. They didn't ask me to sign up; no one pressured me to join. I was a part of it … simply by choosing to walk through the door.

As I became involved with the Program Council, Central started to become the dream I had hoped it to be. The people in and on the council became my friends and my family away from home. The individuals I met through the council helped me open other doors on campus – like the one that led to the drama department, where I danced in a show, or the door that led to the Dean of Students office, where I sat many days, just talking to the Dean, who I affectionately started calling "Papi". My world grew from a small, single dorm room to a microcosm filled with opportunities and optimism. Soon, that small school in Florida became a distant memory and Central became my world. I walked around campus for the next 3 years, just glowing with pride and joy. Pride that I helped make things happen on campus and joy that I felt a part of the college community, filled me on a daily basis.

When it came time to graduate three years later, the class included several members of the Program Council. And though we couldn't sit together, we were bonded together. That's what the Program Council did – it made us one. I would never be alone again because there would always be a door in my heart that led me right back to them.

Courage
doesn't always roar.
Sometimes
courage is the quiet
voice at the end of
the day saying,
"I will try again
tomorrow."

-Mary Anne Rodmacher

Sacred Work
By Duane Brown

I worked for a man several years ago who is probably the best boss, leader really, I will ever work for. He has put in nearly 40 years at the university and his wisdom is priceless. I say this because he taught me something special about the work we do in serving students. Simply put: he called it "sacred work". At first I thought this was cheesy and overly spiritual, I mean, who likes their job that much anyway? Cheesy or not, it didn't take long to realize that the work I do, we all do, in serving students is truly sacred work.

If you are currently a student who is reading this, you share something with every other student on every other campus all over the world: your time's running out. Whether you're a first semester freshman or a seventeenth year senior, eventually you will walk across that platform, receive your hard-earned degree, and say goodbye to your undergraduate years. Trust me, it's coming, and trust me when I say you still have plenty of time to make the most of your experiences.

This is especially true for you, the student programmer. Week after week, you spend your time planning events for your fellow students. You are busy making phone calls, booking hotel rooms and flights, hanging flyers, talking up events, and creating venues out of the most unlikely places like cafeterias, dorm lobbies and laundry rooms (yes, even laundry rooms). You put in the extra hours, and the blood, sweat and tears, to ensure students on your campus are getting countless opportunities to get involved on campus. And the fact of the matter is that we rarely see the benefits of our work in individual students. Sure, we track attendance numbers and measure outcomes, but what do we know of the individual students who attend our events?

Before you read any further in this book, or proceed any further in planning your next event, I want you to know this: the work you are doing is making a difference. You may never hear back from the individual student him- or herself, but what you are accomplishing on your campus is nothing short of miraculous. You are creating opportunities where students are learning more about the people and cultures around them. You are creating opportunities for students to delve deeper into their education. You are creating opportunities for students to simply take a break from a hectic schedule. You are creating opportunities for students to make new friends and maybe even a lifelong love.

You are creating experiences. Experiences that change lives.

You are creating life for the students around you. Never forget that as you program events for those around you. You are doing spectacular things. Thank you for making a difference for students. You are truly doing sacred work.

Becoming A Better Me
By Anne Ritchie

"You have always been a big fish in a small pond." This is one of the last things my dad said to me as he and the rest of my family dropped me off in the parking lot outside of my freshman dorm on my very first day of college at the University of New Hampshire. "And now you are a tiny fish in a huge pond. You have so much room to grow!" Honestly, the last thing that was on my mind that day was some philosophical rambling about fish. I was more concerned with the fact that my new roommate took up the majority of space in the tiny dorm room or the fact that there was no one who knew who I was or where I came from. I was shy and too scared to get to know anyone. That night, I went to bed early while the other freshmen were seeing which fraternity houses threw the best parties. I didn't know who I was or what I was doing at such a big university. I had no major, no friends and no idea what I was going to do.

Over the next several months I did make friends and begin to feel more confident. More people knew my name and most of my professors seemed to know and really like me. I got involved with events in my dorm but still didn't have anything that I could really get my hands on. In high school, I was a girl involved with every club, sport, or extracurricular activity I could find. But how come at college all I seemed to be doing was going to a few classes and staying up way too late watching MTV reality shows?

As the semesters passed, I finally found what I was looking for. I was talking to my RA one afternoon about how I wanted to live on campus throughout the summer. She mentioned to me that I should look into becoming a Freshmen Orientation Leader. I met with past Orientation Leaders and got more information about it. I loved the energy and enthusiasm that these students and my RA had for this program and decided to apply. I prepared myself to help hundreds of incoming freshmen get adjusted to life at the University of New Hampshire. I always considered myself a pretty outgoing person and I liked leading groups, so I knew this was going to be something that I could do to help the university, help other students, and help myself. When I did this, I had no idea that this summer would be one of the best, most fun, and would be made up of activities that would change how I would look at my college experience for many years.

Standing in front of a group of scared, but often rambunctious fresh high school graduates was nothing less than frightening, but with all of that pressure to lead so many students who are looking to be lead, there was no room for me to break under pressure. I was forced to talk louder than I normally would, answer an enormous amount of questions from academics to alcohol, and be one of the people that literally thousands of others people were depending on for help.

This taught me that what I do, what I say and how I act can seriously impact how and what others say and do. I knew, after I oriented my first two groups of freshmen, that there was so much responsibility resting on my shoulders. I was a direct representation of the university and everything I did was a direct reflection on not only my own character, but how the University of New Hampshire shaped me.

Being a student leader that summer showed me that I was much more capable than what I gave myself credit for. I saw that if I never pushed myself, if I never went to a bigger school, never forced myself to make friends or even involve myself in any activities I would never have realized what I was capable of. I was able to meet other students feeling the same was as I did when they got to school for the first time, feel comfortable and capable, even though they were in a totally new place.

When I realized this, I thought back to how my dad told me I needed to grow, and that I would at college. I thought back to how I thought he was only talking about me. I thought he meant I needed to do well in my classes, make a few friends and be respectful of them, and find a career that would satisfy me. After being an Orientation Leader, I realized that he wasn't talking about me. He wanted me to see that as a student leader, I could show others, and more importantly myself what I was capable of. I needed to push my personal boundaries and challenge myself to become a better me, a much bigger fish.

WHERE YOU ARE

IS WHY YOU ARE WHO YOU ARE

-JOE URBANSKI

Leadership is About Purpose, Not Position
By Jack Gottlieb

It is the fall semester of 1998 and I had become President of the Association of Campus Events (ACE). I was extremely excited for myself and about the impact that I could have on Kutztown University. Just that past semester, we had to impeach the previous president due to lack of commitment, leadership and integrity. We suffered that semester, but action had to be taken. I was elected Vice President at the end of that semester. However, the new president pulled out and as a result I assumed the position over that summer. I was nervous and made sure over that summer that I would work hard at everything from honing my leadership skills to learning Parliamentary procedure.

Over Labor Day weekend, I broke my ankle and I knew that the semester would be more difficult for me in general, let alone being a leader within ACE. There were many pressures and challenges to overcome from the board, including the negativity that was left over from last semester. I was so caught up in trying to be a great President that I lost sight of the purpose and focus I wanted to have with everyone. There were many times I spent with my advisor and grad assistants in conflict and challenges on how to lead ACE and its members. There were perceptions that people were starting to view me as they did our last president. So I continued to focus on learning the leadership role and becoming more effective.

It was a Friday night, mid-fall semester, and I was responsible for one of the acts that was part of our huge weekend of programming. Due to the broken ankle, I was taking medicine to help with the pain and decided that night that I would get there a little later so I could rest, thinking, "As President I can do this, and it should not be a big deal". When I arrived at the event, my executive board was furious and I could not understand why. The event was a great success but later reality hit me.

I realized that I got caught up in my title and position and forgot about really focusing on the purpose for which I had gotten involved. Now I was struck that I had been protecting myself rather than putting the group first. From that point on, I became more open and connected to everyone, as people, not just board members. I made sure that whether it was a big event or small event, I would never take for granted the responsibility of this position or the support from the members.

In life, along with our roles on our programming boards, our position titles mean a lot internally. They help us make decisions, follow through on responsibility and guide us to whom to look in times of opportunity and conflict. However, once you leave the walls of that organization, your position title is no longer as important. What is important is the purpose you want to create for your fellow students and campus. So remember that whether you're an executive board member, chairperson or just a board member, that leadership is about purpose, not position.

A Funny Thing Happened On The Way To The Event
By Gary Tuerack

We all have a comfort zone where we like to live. There are certain patterns we walk within . . . cereal we usually eat for breakfast, types of clothes we like to wear, people we feel comfortable connecting with . . . and excuses we make for why we can't step outside our little area. We try to tell ourselves there are reasons that something won't work, but in reality they're excuses! We often have internal dialogues, and start making excuses to ourselves as to why we can't achieve something, why it's wrong to ask that question, or why it's just too darn scary to take a certain action. So here is one of the Secrets of the World's Most Successful People: If you're wondering if it's an excuse, it's an excuse! Another secret that ties together with that one: If you're sweating about a decision, do the thing you're sweating about. Put simply, if the choice is hard and you're making excuses about why you can't or shouldn't do something, put that all aside and just go for it! Combine these two concepts with a few others, and you start doing something I call "Living on the Edge". You will be absolutely amazed at what you will accomplish when you let go of fear, ditch the excuses, and take the actions that make you sweat. And of course, these accomplishments aren't all going to be life altering, super serious or scary! An example from my own life:

In my role as a motivational speaker I travel frequently. This affords me wonderful opportunities to meet amazing new people, and of course the change to focus on overcoming challenges as they arise while I'm outside my comfort zone – so I'm focusing on living on the edge. A few years back I had an experience that has stuck with me – and probably also my audience that night! – I would like to share.

Before this particular show, I was running around like a nut trying to get everything ready on time. They had a small room behind the stage for me to keep my things and do all my prep work in, so I was in and out of there a few times filling water-balloons and grabbing some other props. Right before I was supposed to do my presentation (I could hear applause coming from the audience for the guy before me), I realized I had to go to the bathroom. So I let my host know I was running to the back again for a quick second, went into the bathroom and shut the door behind me. When I was ready to head back out and jog onto stage, I grabbed the door handle and twisted – but it didn't budge. I pulled, I tugged, I yanked, I tried to bust through, but still nothing moved. The door had locked behind me and I was stuck inside! You can imagine my standing there banging on the door screaming for the host: "Amy! I gotta get ready for the show!" But no one was coming to let me out.

At that point I could have just gotten frustrated, admitted defeat and waited for someone to figure out why I wasn't showing up for my presentation. But I'm committed to living on the edge, right? No excuses! So I looked in the mirror and just thought to myself: "Now, this is funny. What do I do? She's not coming back, and it's the program start time." I started looking around this little room I was locked in, and I realized they had those removable ceiling tiles with the metal pieces in between them. So I climbed on to the toilet, then on to the sink, and reached up to pry out a ceiling tile and pulled myself up to take a look around. I was feeling a little like James Bond at this point - there were wires and duct pieces everywhere and I was going to have to try and get through all that stuff. But I thought, "It's just one room over. I've never climbed through a ceiling before, but how tough can it be? Am I going to live on the edge?" So after looking around a bit, I actually climbed up into the ceiling, walked on the metal pieces in between the tiles and squeezed myself over to the next room where I could climb down. And I made it to the program. So, incidentally, did a big piece of ceiling tile, which became my new prop to show the audience how living on the edge enables you to do things you would never have thought to do before.

After you live on the edge for a few experiences, your comfort zone begins to grow so wide that you can suddenly do things you would have talked yourself out of in the past. Is it possible I might have gotten hurt crawling through the ceiling? Sure, but I took all reasonable caution I could, and then took a risk. That's living on the edge, and that's how you get the amazing experiences that so many of us want in our lives.

Editor's Note: For more information on Gary Teurack, please visit
www.societyofsuccess.com

don't
MAJOR
in
MINOR
things.

— Anthony J. D'Angelo

Semper Gumby!
By Anthony J. D'Angelo

I remember the day like it was yesterday. I arrived at the Student Center at Rowan University in Glassboro, New Jersey. It was about two hours before show time and I saw members of the Student Activities Board working together to ensure that all of the AV was ready to go for the annual leadership conference which I would be helping to kick off.

Then something very unique caught my eye. It was those black t-shirts. Now I've seen literally seen hundreds of program board t-shirts before in my travels to college campuses across the country. But never before have I seen black t-shirts like these.

As I approached the group to make my introduction one older looking student turned to me and said, "Hello Sir! Welcome to Rowan University! My name is Robert."

I could tell by Robert's introduction and by the crew cut he sported that he obviously had a military background. But before I could say anything my eyes caught those black t-shirts again. Now I could see what was on them. The black t-shirts had the image of a green Gumby and the slogan "Semper Gumby" on the front.

"Hello Robert. My name is Tony D'Angelo. Thanks for having me on campus today. I look forward to serving you and the Rowan Community. By the way, I love your shirts, but I have to ask what does Semper Gumby mean? I know that the marine motto is Semper Fidelis, which means Always Be Faithful. But what the heck is Semper Gumby?" I asked.

"Sir" Robert barked. "Before I came to Rowan, I served in the United States Marine Corp sir. It is in fact correct that our official motto is Semper Fidelis. However the unofficial motto of the United States Marine Corp is Semper Gumby."

"I got it Robert. But what the heck does Semper Gumby mean?" I pushed.

"Sir, for me, being in student programming is like being in the marines. You never know what might go wrong and when it might go wrong, but you have to face the fact that things will go wrong. Hence we say Semper Gumby!" chided Robert.

"Okay I give up!" I said. "What does Semper Gumby mean? Always be Green!?"

"No sir. I've come to learn that you never know when the shit is going to hit the fan when you are putting on events here on campus. Semper Gumby means, Always Be Flexible. Just like Gumby sir!" Robert said with a grin on his face and a twinkle in his eye.

"Semper Gumby Robert!" I said as I gave Robert a high five.

Seven Programming Tips for Events
By Will Keim, PhD

The Seven Programming Tips have been designed to help you make your program a success. These tips have evolved from working with hundreds of thousands of students from hundreds of campuses in North America. A GOOD PROGRAM WILL RESULT FROM GOOD PROGRAM PLANNING!

1. Get Right to the Basics - You can never book too early, but there are a few things to check:

> o Set a date and time of event.
>
> o Does date conflict with school, state or national programs? (Example: Monday Night football, school sporting event, or other keynote lectures on campus, etc).
>
> o Put date on campus calendar and give date to campus information office.

2. Secure the Budget - Funding is always possible if you utilize all resources on campus

> o Is funding approved?
>
> o If short of funds, which other groups on campus could contribute?
>
> o Is there university paperwork to finalize payment to performers?

3. Reserve the Building - This may be one of the hardest tasks to complete if you wait too long.

> o Reserve building with official papers signed.
>
> o Reserve wireless microphone.
>
> o Check quality of sound
>
> o Decide on lighting and seating arrangements.

4. Delegate Your Tasks - Have the planning committee divide into

subgroups for efficiency and to facilitate Ownership and Involvement. Subgroups could involve:
  o Equipment/Room Coordinator
  o Publicity
      a. general public
      b. specialized groups (Fraternities, Sororities, Residence Halls, Ethnic and Independent groups)
      c. Recommend a representative per each large student organization to be on publicity committee
  o Coordinator of travel/lodging
  o Reception Coordinator
  o Theme/Topic Coordinator
5. Make a Timeline - Having a timeline for publicity helps to utilize all resources. The 45-day plan has proven very successful
    a. 30 - 45 days before event
        • Have representative go to large student group meeting to personally tell about event and how they can get involved. Pick excited well-informed representatives to go to these meetings.
    b. 15 - 30 days before event
        • Large posters out
        • Article of interest in local/school newspaper
        • Plan creative types of publicity. Put a plan out to the public every four to five days during this period (see # 6)
    c. 7 - 15 days before event
        • Final reminders by representative to push the event by word of mouth the last week.
        • Follow-up with each student organization.
    d. Last 7 days
        • Ads in local/school newspapers
        • Large banners in strategic locations

- Final small flyers
- Public announcements on radio/TV
6. Publicize, Publicize, Publicize - A summary of the most popular avenues of publicity.
    o Campus Activities Office
    o Student newspaper
    o Town newspaper
    o Radio/TV stations
    o Faculty/Senate announcement
    o Student Government Association
    o Residence Hall Association
    o Table Tents
    o Souvenir items; buttons, t-shirts, etc.
    o Display cases
    o Banners
    o Flyers, posters
    o Special invitations to campus/community dignitaries
    o Facebook/Myspace
    o WORD OF MOUTH!!!
7. Evaluation - The evaluation is often forgotten and one of the most useful tools for future successes.
    o Feedback sheets at the event
    o Follow-up meeting for feedback with planning group members
    o Answer the following questions:
        1. Was the event a success? (Define what a success means to your group?
        2. Did it meet the original need?
        3. Was the event cost effective?

Editor's Note: For more information on Will Keim, please visit www.willkeim.com

Does Size Really Matter?

By Jen Bothwell

It's not the size of your program board;
It's not the size of your budget;
It's not the size of your audience;
It's not the size of your free t-shirt stash;
It's not the size of your programming calendar that matters.

What matters is that you wake up every day excited
about what you are doing for your campus.

It matters that you make a difference
within your college community.

And at the end of the day, if you love what you do,
then that is all that really matters.

Follow Your Yellow Brick Road
By Stephanie Russell Holz

The Wizard of Oz is one of my favorite movies, and it often helps me put what I do in perspective. I believe that students come to college on a journey just like Dorothy. They are submerged in a culture of new traditions, different populations, and amazing opportunities. As students follow the yellow brick road, they gain life skills along the way through their involvement in campus activities.

Just as the Scarecrow was looking for a brain, students are looking to expand their minds with new ideas. As advisors it is our job to help students relate what they are doing in the classroom to their co-curricular involvement. We challenge them to think outside of the box. We encourage them to think creatively and to problem solve. We help them come to decisions on their own. Through thought provoking and educational programming, we expand their minds.

In the Wizard of Oz, the Tin Man was looking for a heart. I think as advisors it is our job to help students lead with heart. Many students who come to college initially take on leadership roles for position or power. As they continue on the yellow brick road, it is our goal that they put this notion aside and realize the importance of mentoring and leading by example. We help students find what they are passionate about so when they do lead, they are leading for the right reasons. As advisors we help them find their heart by serving as mentors, by rewarding them when they lead with heart, and by providing resources to them.

Inspiration for Student Programmers

The Cowardly Lion was looking for courage on his way to the Emerald City. I believe campus activities provide students with many opportunities to be courageous and to gain confidence in their abilities. I have witnessed timid first year students come into my office at the start of their college careers. Four years later, after being a leader in a campus organization, they are transformed into a different person. They are confident in their abilities because of the leadership experiences they have had. Because of these experiences they are able to stand up for what they believe in. They have the courage to voice their opinions when it is not in line with the majority. They are more aware of different cultures and populations, and they appreciate those differences. They have the courage they need to be successful.

I see the Advisor as the Wizard. While students would like us to be the "all powerful" Oz and give them the answers to all of their questions, we choose to be more like the little man behind the curtain. We equip them with the tools they need to be successful by serving as a resource, mentor, challenger, support, friend, and advisor. Our goal is that they discover the Emerald City on their own because only then does true learning take place.

Dorothy and her friends made it all the way to the Emerald City to see the Wizard and were quite disappointed when the Wizard turned out to be a fraud and could not solve all their problems. However, it turns out that through their journey the Scarecrow already had gained a brain, the Tin Man a heart, and the Lion courage. I believe this is how campus activities work for students. Students do not realize all the skills they are gaining through being involved in campus activities or through attending campus programs. The learning is the journey itself.

Are You Hauling Buckets Or Building A Pipeline?
By Jack Gottlieb

We have two offices at Collegiate EmPowerment. Our team center is located in the prestigious college town of Princeton, New Jersey. Our second office- our creative studio is located in the lesser known yet quite historic college town of Easton, Pennsylvania. The creative studio is located in the same building complex which houses both the Crayola® Crayon Factory and the National Canal Museum.

In addition to having lots of cool crayons, we also have a great opportunity to learn about the rich history of our second home city. The roots of history run deep in Easton. On a recent break from work, the curator of the National Canal Museum shared this local lore with us...

Once upon a time, when Easton was just a small village on the banks of a fine, clear Delaware River, the villagers all drew their water from the river, and used it to cook, and bathe and water their gardens. Life was good.

During one particular rainy season, the river flooded. When the water went down, the river had cut itself a new channel, far from the village. The wise village elders conferred and decided to hire someone to supply the village with water. Two villagers stepped forward and asked for the water contract. The village elders decided that a little competition might be a good thing, and issued both villagers a contract.

The first villager, John the Wise, took the new water contract and left the village, saying he would return to the village with great amounts of clear water. It would be many weeks before the villagers again saw John the Wise. The other villager, Eli the Strong, seeing that he was the only one with a water contract, bought two shiny new buckets and set to work. Every day, Eli would take a bucket in each hand, walk to the river, fill his buckets, and walk back to the village. The villagers would all come and take some of Eli's water and pay him for it. Eli the Strong was happy.

Soon, however, the villagers wanted more water than Eli could carry in his two buckets. So Eli started making two trips a day, and doubled the amount of money coming in. Eli's wife was happy. Again, the villagers soon demanded more water. So, being Eli the Strong after all, Eli fashioned a yoke for his back and bought two additional buckets. Eli could now carry four buckets of water on each round trip, and again the money coming into the Strong household doubled. Each time the villagers demanded more water, Eli would come up with a way to make more trips to the river, and carry more buckets on each trip. Eventually, Eli could do no more and spent every waking moment on the road between the village and the river.

About this time, John the Wise returned. He surveyed the land around the village and made arrangements to cross some of the villagers' fields. He started laying down strange tubes, making one long tube from the river all the way to the village. John would stand on the river bank with his bucket, and scoop water from the river into the tube. The water would run down the tube, and into a tank John built at the edge of the village. Soon the village became accustomed to getting their water from John's tank when they wanted it, and stopped waiting for Eli the Strong. Soon Eli the

Strong had to fold up his business, for there were no customers for his water.

John the Wise then hired Eli the Strong, giving him the money from every tenth bucket. Once John trusted Eli to continue pouring water into the tube, he disappeared again.

This time, when John the Wise returned, he constructed a strange wheel-like machine that turned in the river's current. With each turn of the wheel, water poured from the scoops on the wheel into the tube, so no one need stand and labor. The villagers had clear water whenever they desired, and in any quantity.

Are You Hauling Buckets Or Building A Pipeline?

In other words, are you only doing one shot, onetime events and programs or are you creating a culture of impact for your campus community? The choice is yours.

Editor's Note: Jack Gottlieb serves as the Executive Director for Campus Impact Initiatives at Collegiate EmPowerment. Campus Impact Initiatives is an ongoing consultation experience with Collegiate EmPowerment. It is designed to help campus communities transform their programming efforts & activities into meaningful and lasting experiences for today's college student.

HOPE

S FOR PEOPLE WHO DON'T KNOW WHAT TO EXPECT

- JOE URBANSKI

The Coin Of Indecision
By Sean Adams

There comes a time in everyone's life when they must make a hard decision. I have found there is one way to ensure that you make a decision you are emotionally comfortable with at a gut level. Begin by narrowing your ideas down to two different options. Assign one option to heads and one option to tails. Now, and this is the hard part, flip the coin. It does not matter if you flip it and catch it turning it over on the back of your other hand, or letting it land and seeing how it landed, etc. Just flip it, there are no minimum numbers or rotations the coin must reach for this process to work, you just need to get the coin moving in some way. Now, look at the coin. If it is heads, ask yourself how you feel about the decision you assigned to heads. If it is tails, do the same for the decision you assigned to tails. The blessing of this technique is that it forces you to have an emotional reaction to the decision that was made for you. You no longer have the stress of making the decision; the coin did it for you. All you have to do is emotionally react.

For example, you are deciding between moving to Chicago or Boston. You have made the lists of pros and cons for each, and you cannot decide. So you assign heads to Chicago and tails to Boston. (Or vice versa, it does not matter.). Once you have heads for Chicago and tails for Boston, you flip the coin. For this example, the coin comes up tails. How do you feel about moving to Boston? If you feel a lightening or simple joy, then you know that it is the right decision. If you feel a clenching in your stomach, either strong or mild, then your body is telling you that it is uncomfortable with that decision.

The coin does not make the decision for you; it simply forces you to have to make an emotional reaction to a decision that was made. This is important because to be a truly good leader we must learn to trust our gut and know it has the wisdom and guidance we need.

A New Tradition Starts Somewhere
By Erin Morrell, M.A.

Even though I have only been in the field for a few years, I
certainly have many stories of programs that went well and those
that did not. One of my favorite memories is from when I was in
graduate school and served as a Graduate Assistant in the Office
of Student Activities at Fairfield University. One of my mentors
there challenged each of the graduate assistants to leave their own
personal legacy behind for future students to enjoy. This was
something that I really wanted to do for the Fairfield community.

I tried to think of all of my experiences as a student leader and
even as a typical college student, to think of an idea that would be
memorable. Being a realist (and a programmer), I asked the
question, "how much money do I have to work with?" and my
mentor replied with the following – "You come up with a good
idea, and we will find the money for it." As a grad assistant I
wasn't really sure what to do with that. Should I plan something
elaborate and go for it, or try to be budget conscious and still
invoke a grand idea? After a few weeks, I finally came up with
something that I thought might catch his eye…

At my alma mater, the University of Connecticut, the Division
of Student Affairs hosted a Midnight Breakfast at the end of each
semester immediately before final exams. The best part about this
event (aside from the free food) was the fact that faculty, staff and
administrators came to serve the students and wish them well on
their upcoming exams. It was an event where you ate a great deal,
always left with some snacks for your room for study breaks, and

were able to mingle with other students and administrators all at the same event. It made you temporarily forget that you had some studying to do.

Once I had my idea, I did a little research by contacting some of the administrators that I knew from UConn to help me get an idea of how much money, staffing and work went into the event. I then went and pitched it to my mentor, Vice President for Student Affairs, Jim Fitzpatrick. Mr. Fitzpatrick loved the idea and asked me to coordinate Fairfield's First Annual Midnight Breakfast!

Taking some ideas from the well established UConn Midnight Breakfast and incorporating some Fairfield traditions, I began working on this event. We ordered aprons with the Stag (Fairfield's Mascot) on it, as well as created buttons for the servers to wear. I contacted the faculty, staff and administrators at the university to ask them to participate, and it was well received. Some faculty members even came in their pajamas! We created an event that was so popular that I thought we would run out of food. We didn't really know what to expect for a new event, so we decided to safely plan for a few hundred students. Little did we know that it would be so popular that we had over one thousand students come! The food service staff graciously tapped into their food supplies for breakfast for the upcoming week and we were able to serve everyone.

Working closely with the food service staff and the rest of the staff in the Office of Student Activities, we created an event that is still an annual event at Fairfield. During a recent visit to Fairfield, when I was introduced as a former grad assistant, someone mentioned that I was the one that started the annual Midnight

Breakfast and they smiled and said, "That's awesome."

I have to say that I am proud of the event, not because it was my idea to bring it to Fairfield, but because it has become something that students and administrators look forward to each year. It is now my legacy and a new Fairfield tradition.

What Every College Creed Should Be
By Anthony J. D'Angelo

STUDENTS are...
important people on this campus.

Not cold enrollment statistics, but flesh & blood,
human beings with feeling & emotions like our own.

Not people to be tolerated
so that we can do our thing.

THEY ARE OUR THING.

Not dependent on us.
Rather we are both interdependent upon one another.
Not an interruption of our work,
but the purpose of it.

Without students there would
be no need for this institution.

Editor's Note: This inspiring piece is also available in poster format. If
you are interested in the poster format of this piece please call toll free:
1-877-EDUTAIN (338-8246) or email: info@Collegiate-EmPowerment.org.
Poster prints can also be viewed online at
www.Collegiate-EmPowerment.org.
It makes for the perfect poster to hang on your office door!

Finding Your Voice
Through A Whisper
By Jack Gottlieb

It was August 23, 1997. I had just transferred to Kutztown
University after taking a year off from my first college. I was not
happy there and needed time away to find myself. Once I got to
Kutztown, I was scared like many of us when we go to a new
college, but I felt more connected to who I was and was able to
meet people as myself, not as someone I was trying to be.

After a month I found myself invited to a drive-in movie by
someone who was involved with ACE (Association of Campus
Events). I ended up joining, and before I knew it, I took on the
Comedy Chair position. Then came November 9, 1997.

I had just finished watching the Eagles game and found a message
on my voicemail. It was my grandmother. She proceeded to tell
me that the previous week my father was in a horrific car accident.
He was in a coma and may have to be pulled off life support and
that I had to come home. First of all, yes you read that right, *last
week*. I just remember being in shock because I was as close to my
Dad as anyone could be. I kept pounding on a cement wall with my
fist in disbelief.

I hated many people in my family for not telling me sooner. The
rest of the semester was a blur until he started showing signs that
he was getting better. He briefly came out of the coma, and as a
result, I was able to talk with him, even if he could not talk to me. I
talked to him about the Eagles and fed him ice chips so he could

stay hydrated. Then on December 23, 1997, my Dad passed away. Seeing him throughout that time was very hard, but at the same, time I also felt like I never wanted to leave. When I got the news, it took three hours for it to hit me. I took a shower just to try and collect myself and cried for hours. However, what came through to me at that moment was the motto my father lived by - I will never compromise myself for anyone.

When the spring semester started in 1998, I began a journey that continues to this day. I made sure that through anything I did within my programming board I spoke my mind, and never left anything unsaid. What follows is what I wrote in my journal during the course of my involvement with the programming board:

I will not get caught up in being right, just doing the right thing.
I will not care about looking good, just being real.
I will not take on something unless I know it has a purpose.
I will live for what my dad held true;
freedom of thought and action.
I will not allow fear to hold me back from taking chances.
I will fight for what I believe to be important.
I will allow the voice inside to be heard by others.

Do not go through another moment without sharing the voice you have inside of you, because when you do, you find more within yourself and others.

The Boy Under The Tree
By David Coleman and Kevin Randall

In the summer break between my freshman and sophomore years in college, I was invited to be an instructor at a high school leadership camp hosted by a college in Michigan. I was already highly involved in most campus activities, and I jumped at the opportunity.

About an hour into the first day of camp, amid the frenzy of icebreakers and forced interactions, I first noticed the boy under the tree. He was small and skinny, and his obvious discomfort and shyness made him appear frail and fragile. Only 50 feet away, 200 eager campers were bumping bodies, playing, joking and meeting each other, but the boy under the tree seemed to want to be anywhere other than where he was. The desperate loneliness he radiated almost stopped me from approaching him, but I remembered the instructions from the senior staff to stay alert for campers who might feel left out.

As I walked toward him I said, "Hi, my name is Kevin and I'm one of the counselors. It's nice to meet you. How are you?" In a shaky, sheepish voice he reluctantly answered, "Okay, I guess" I calmly asked him if he wanted to join the activities and meet some new people. He quietly replied, "No, this is not really my thing."

I could sense that he was in a new world, that this whole experience was foreign to him. But I somehow knew it wouldn't be right to push him, either. He didn't need a pep talk, he needed a friend. After several silent moments, my first interaction with the boy under the tree was over.

At lunch the next day, I found myself leading camp songs at the top of my lungs for two hundred of my new friends. The campers eagerly participated. My gaze wandered over the mass of noise and movement and was caught by the image of the boy from under the tree, sitting alone, staring out the window. I nearly forgot the words to the song I was supposed to be leading.

At my first opportunity, I tried again, with the same questions as before: "How are you doing? Are you okay?" To which he again replied, "Yeah, I'm alright. I just don't really get into this stuff." As I left the cafeteria, I too realized this was going to take more time and effort than I had thought -- if it was even possible to get through to him at all.

That evening at our nightly staff meeting, I made my concerns about him known. I explained to my fellow staff members my impression of him and asked them to pay special attention and spend time with him when they could. The days I spend at camp each year fly by faster than any others I have known. Thus, before I knew it, mid-week had dissolved into the final night of camp and I was chaperoning the "last dance." The students were doing all they could to savor every last moment with their new "best friends" -- friends they would probably never see again.

As I watched the campers share their parting moments, I suddenly saw what would be one of the most vivid memories of my life. The boy from under the tree, who stared blankly out the kitchen window, was now a shirtless dancing wonder. He owned the dance floor as he and two girls proceeded to cut up a rug. I watched as he shared meaningful, intimate time with people at whom he couldn't even look at just days earlier. I couldn't believe it was the same person.

In October of my sophomore year, a late-night phone call pulled me away from my chemistry book. A soft-spoken, unfamiliar voice asked politely, "Is Kevin there?"

"You're talking to him. Who's this?"

"This is Tom Johnson's mom. Do you remember Tommy from leadership camp?

The boy under the tree. How could I not remember?

"Yes, I do," I said. "He's a very nice young man. How is he?"

An abnormally long pause followed, and then Mrs. Johnson said, "My Tommy was walking home from school this week when he was hit by a car and killed." Shocked, I offered my condolences. "I just wanted to call you," she said, "because Tommy mentioned you so many times. I wanted you to know that he went back to school this fall with confidence. He made new friends. His grades went up. And he even went out on a few dates. I just wanted to thank you for making a difference for Tom. The last few months were the best few months of his life."

In that instant, I realized how easy it is to give a bit of yourself every day. You may never know how much each gesture may mean to someone else. I tell this story as often as I can, and when I do, I urge others to look out for their own "boy under the tree."

Editor's Note: David Coleman is known as "The Dating Doctor" and "America's Real-Life Hitch!" He has appeared on 2,500 campuses speaking to more than two million students, parents, faculty and staff and is known for his engaging stage presence. Honored TEN TIMES as the National Campus Speaker of the Year, David is also the Founder and President of Coleman Productions, one of the most successful speaker agencies in America. For further information on David Coleman, visit www.datingdoctor.com

Nothing will work
unless you do.

-Maya Angelou

Rainbow Flag Number 7
By Ken Schneck

I was never a student programmer.
I was never an activist.
I was never an educator.

I'm gay. I date men. End of story.

Junior year of college.
I'm an RA.

I put a rainbow flag on my door.
It gets torn down.
Damn it.

I buy another rainbow flag and put it on my door.
Someone writes all over it with a black marker.
Damn it.

I buy another rainbow flag and put it on my door.
It gets torn down.
Damn it all to hell.

Pretty soon, the man behind the counter in the rainbow flag store
Smiles when he sees me coming.
I think I'm keeping the rainbow flag store in business.

Flag Four disappeared.

"FAG" was written on Flag Five.
I think Flag Six just got nervous and skipped away.
Then Rainbow Flag Seven goes up.

I wait for it to get torn down.
Rainbow Flag Seven stays up.

I wait for the black marker.
Rainbow Flag Seven stays clean.

I wait for "FAG".
Rainbow Flag Seven scoffs.

The rainbow flag store waits for me to keep them in business.
I never had to go back.

Somewhere in the waiting,
I realized I'm a student programmer.
I realized I'm an activist.
I realized I'm an educator.

I don't campaign.
I don't lobby.
I don't raise money.

I just have a flag.
Rainbow Flag Seven.
Still hanging proud on my door.

Mr. Frigid
By Robert J. Kerr

While attending Graduate School at Colorado State, I was introduced to the Men's Movement and Mr. Warren Farrel. Warren was brought to campus in the spring of my first year to work with us on increasing the sensitivity of males to the rest of the world. As I worked with the fraternity community, it was part of my job to participate in the program.

The first program was an all school program in one of the bigger ballrooms. The title of the program was billed as "Mr. America Pageant" and I thought it might be interesting. Little did I know that it would soon become a heated competition that still leaves vivid memories on my mind and taught me lessons I have never forgotten.

While the evening started innocently enough, it soon turned to something more interactive. All the males were brought to the stage and lined up. Then, by applause Warren would determine who the six finalists would be for the formal contest. Well, as luck would have there were a significant number of sorority women in the audience who I knew, from my work, that I was doomed. Sure enough, when the selection process was over I was one of the six and headed backstage to prepare for the contest.

When we were safely behind the curtain, Warren came back and handed out Speedo swimsuits and sashes for everyone. I was given Mr. Alaska/Mr. Frigid and a Speedo suit I would never have worn in public. I looked at the other five contestants as they held up their skimpy suits and slid their sashes over the head and we all let out a collective sigh as we began to strip down so we could put on the swim suits. Ultimately, we all stood there in our Speedos holding our hands in front of us and kind of giggling at our fate.

When Warren had us come out from behind the curtain we were greeted with catcalls and whistles. Blushing and feeling naked, I stood there and wondered how long this contest would take. The first thing Warren had us do was parade through a lineup of the women by leaving the stage and walking in front and then returning to the stage. While we paraded around, the women were allowed to pinch, squeeze and touch anywhere they wanted. I don't know about anybody else but I quickly became very competitive. It was if I wanted to be the one that got the most pinches. While this process began to ease the discomfort we felt, it quickly accelerated the urge to win. After all, we were being embarrassed enough so we might as well get serious about this and focus on winning.

When we got back to the stage, Warren introduced us to the second phase of the contest – the talent competition. I think we all looked at each other and began to feel trapped and lost. The first contestant sprinted across the stage and then ran a fast lap around the inside of the ballroom. As he returned to the stage, the women applauded him and he smiled and took a bow. The second contestant recited a poem, a simple childhood poem, and I was frustrated because I was going to recite a poem and felt that now I must do something else. As Warren approached me, I did the only thing that came to my mind. I spoke a basic greeting and response in Russian, pretty much all that I remembered from my senior year Russian class. When it was over, I got howls and applause as well. That's when I figured out if you did anything you were going to get support from the crowd.

At last, we came to the last phase of the contest. We would each be asked a question and would answer in the spirit of our title. Since I was Mr. Frigid, I thought it would be fairly simple. What I also began to notice was that none of us appeared self-conscious in our skimpy swimsuits. In fact we would often strike poses and play to the crowd. Fascinating since a mere twenty minutes earlier we were all very ill at ease with the tight and very revealing swimsuits. Now, we unabashedly displayed ourselves and were eager for the positive responses.

When the questions were asked, mine was how did I feel about pre-marital sex. I answered in character and expressed my concern for how the young lady would think of me and if she would respect me. That brought the house down. I was feeling very strong. I felt I had a chance of winning the contest. To my surprise, I actually had thoughts about winning. In fact, it was becoming important to me that I do well in the contest.

After all the contestants answered their questions, we paraded around the stage one more time and waited for the voting. Warren had a simple way of voting; he merely held his hand over someone's head and listened to the applause. Based on this process, I finished third of six and don't really remember much about the winner. In fact, as we all went back stage to change, I heard guys grumbling that they thought they would have fared better in the voting. I was amazed, because I felt the same way. In only thirty minutes, we had gone from shy, embarrassed college guys to fiery competitors who wanted another shot at the title.

I learned a lot about how women can feel when men stare at them and make remarks about how they look, move and act. Also that we all yearn for acceptance and praise, sometimes at any cost.

ALL OF THE
OBSTACLES
IN YOUR LIFE ARE THE
BUILDING BLOCKS
OF YOUR FUTURE
SUCCESS

-ANTHONY J. D'ANGELO

What It Means To Be A Programmer
By Joe Urbanski

You are part of a team of student leaders on campus.
You live in the student activities office,
and you have your own couch.
You secretly wrote your name on the bottom of it,
in case anyone asks.
You sometimes sleep on it too.

You build confidence and increase your capacity for greatness.
You have the ability to change students' lives through your events.
You endure challenges non-involved students
would never understand.
You laugh, you cry, you question, and you live like never before.

You leave class early to set up for events three hours in advance.
You skip sleep on the weekends
just to party the non-alcoholic way.
You get calls on your cell phone from celebrities,
or at least their agents.
You have access to the entertainment industry at your fingertips.

You sometimes suffer through the worst events ever.
You program for everyone and no one shows up.
You program for everyone and the performer doesn't show up.
You program for everyone and get none of the credit.

You also get to experience the best events ever.
You see your favorite performers and the campus pays for it.
You influence $50,000 decisions, and sometimes even more.
You have the ability to entertain, educate,
and inspire fellow students.

You realize that programming is about communication.
You begin to communicate internally with your real self.
You understand who you are and what you do at the very core.
You are a programmer.

The Rock Star Treatment
By Anthony D'Angelo

As a student activities programmer/professional, never doubt the impact that you will have on the performers and speakers you bring to your campus. When in fact, your intention is to have the performer impact your campus, don't forget that your actions will inevitably impact the performer as well. Here's my story of how one such professional impacted me:

It was the Fall of 1997, and I was on my very first "real" college speaking tour to promote my first book, "The College Blue Book." At this point, I was a total rookie and knew nothing. I had spent the first two years of my career trying to break into the college market as a motivational speaker by working with Greek and RA communities, but the opportunities were too few and trying to connect with a bunch of drunken guys during Greek Week just wasn't my thing. I did however have the opportunity to reach an extraordinary number of college students (+250,000 from over 500 schools) during my first two years, but something was missing. I loved serving the students but I was missing a connection with the professionals whom I served.

You see, up until this point in my career I did not know about NACA and the amazing profession of Campus Activities. I was accustomed to working with well meaning, yet professionally incompetent people who attempted to slap together last minute programs with little planning and insight on what it truly takes to create a successful event. I vividly recall hundreds of times in which I would arrive at a campus and there would be no seating, no microphone, no handouts, no promotional efforts, no check and often the "professional" who was supposed to greet me never even showed up to the event. This was the norm for me for over two years and then I met Kristen.

Kristen was a graduate student at Shippensburg University studying under the legendary student affairs guru Jan Arminio. As part of her graduate work, Kristen worked in the office of new student orientation and helped to coordinate opening weekend. I was slated to be the keynote speaker for the kickoff to new student orientation at Shippensburg University. Kristen was my contact on campus.

Growing up in south central Pennsylvania, I knew all about SHIP (that's what we called Shippensburg U). As a matter of fact, three members of my family attended SHIP as well as 10 members of my graduating class at Cedar Cliff high school. Even though I was quite familiar with the campus and the culture, I was still nervous about making my debut at SHIP. Then I met Kristen…

It was a typical hazy, hot and humid August day when I stepped into the cool air conditioned auditorium. My mind was in a funk, not only because of the drastic change in temperature, but also by the fact that SHIP was taking orientation seriously; as my experience with most campuses up until this point was having orientation hosted in a hot, sweaty, cavernous gymnasium. "Pretty cool." I thought to myself.

Amidst the sweet smell of a peppermint-like fragrance, I heard the sound of Vivaldi's Four Seasons over the house sound system as I gazed towards the warmly lit stage. "Was I in the right place?" I thought to myself. "This seems more like opening night versus

New Student Orientation. SHIP is doing this right!"

"Hi Tony! Welcome to Shippensburg!" a peppy voice said from the stage. It took a moment for my eyes to focus due to the soft lights and then I saw her smile. It was Kristen.

"My name is Kristen Bendon and I am here to assist you today. Thank you for being here to help make new student orientation a success. We are glad to have you here as a guest. If there is anything that I can do for you, just let me know. Please allow me to show you to your dressing room."

Shock! Joy! Happiness! I felt like a Rock star. I simply uttered, "This is so cool! I have a dressing room!"

"Of course! We here at Shippensburg are a class act!" Kristen said.

"You are indeed!" I conferred.

Kristen led me backstage down a long hallway. There before me was a door adorned with 4 colorful balloons and a huge yellow glittery star with my name on it—Guest Speaker—Anthony J. D'Angelo. "Damn! I AM a Rock star!" I thought to myself.

As Kristen swung the door open, a bounty of treasures lay before me. ("Bounty of treasures" is a little dramatic, but then again I had only received a token bottle of luke-warm water from past host clients.) All my favorites where there! Shinny red delicious apples, ripe bananas, a can of Almonds, 4 Zone Bars, chilled water and my absolute favorite type of iced tea- Lipton's Brewed Tea Sweetened- no lemon (the one with the blue label). I was in heaven! I had arrived!

"How in the heck did you know about all of my favorite things Kristen? You must be a psychic!" I exclaimed.

"Actually a little mouse told me, your program manager, Bill, told me about your preferences."

"Well thanks for doing your homework! I really, really appreciate this!" I said.

Then Kristen handed me a lovely decorated gift bag with the Shippensburg University seal on it and said, "This is a token of our appreciation. Thanks again for helping to make orientation a success."

"Thank you!" I said as I opened the gift bag and pulled out a gray XL sweatshirt with the word SHIP emblazed on it.

"This is so cool! I don't know what to say. I have never received a sweatshirt from any of the schools at which I have presented before. This is my very first one! Thank you Kristen. This is so kind of you." As I gave her a hug of appreciation.

"You're welcome." She said with a smile.

"I'll never forget this Kristen."

The opening keynote for new student orientation at Shippensburg University that year went off without a glitch and was no doubt one of my best performances to date. After all how could I let Kristen and her students down after everything she had done to make me feel so important? That night I was truly invested in the success of those students whom I spoke to. Kristen treated me like a Rock star and in return I gave them a Rock Star performance.

It has been over a decade since I first met that young professional named Kristen Bendon. I literally have had the privilege to speak at over 2,200 college campuses across the country since meeting her on that warm August night in central Pennsylvania. I have spoken to over a million college students, worked with over 35,000 student affairs professionals and by now I have enough college sweatshirts to outfit an entire residence hall and I can tell you this-- I may not remember all the faces, nor recall all the places, but there is one thing which I will never forget and that is the way Kristen treated me that night. She made me feel special so I could make her students feel special as well.

By the way, I still have the sweatshirt!

Editor's note: When we first began to develop the co-author team for Inspiration for Student Programmers who, do you think, Tony insisted that we have on our team? That woman named Kristen, who is now known as Kristen Hyman.

FOCUS ON PROGRESS...... NOT PERFECTION......

- DAN SULLIVAN

A Beautiful Mess
By Duane Brown

A friend shared with me a story about a young boy and his grandmother...

A young boy would often stay with his grandmother. They would spend time together sitting in the living room. He would sit on the floor, cross-legged and listen to his grandmother spin tales of her own childhood intertwined with the fairy tales the boy had grown to adore. Hours would pass, and soon the afternoon would fade to dusk. But what the boy remembered more than anything was not the stories or the fairy tales or even the smell of fresh-baked cookies that seemed to always hover like an invisible sweet cloud in his grandmother's home. Rather, his memories were of his view from the floor staring up at his grandmother sitting in her ancient rocker with the brown and green afghan hanging neatly over the back. More dear than all the stories was his grandmother's constant cross-stitching, her hands working tirelessly tying knots lightning fast and working the strings like a skilled surgeon.

From his view, sitting silently on the tasseled floor rug, the back of the cross-stitch frame perplexed the boy. It was a true mess, a catastrophic tangle of knots and mismatched yarn flowing from every direction. None of it made any sense and it was downright ugly. Yet, his grandmother pushed and pulled and tied the strings with artistic precision and all the while creating more of a stringy, tangled mess to the young boy. And each time when she finally put down her tools, she would look down into her grandson's adoring eyes and flip the cross-stitch frame over to reveal a beautiful piece of art held together by a tangled mess of disorder and ugliness on the other side of the canvas.

Often our lives make very little sense to us. Things go wrong, our plans get tangled together, and we get into mismatched relationships that are truly ugly. Seemingly, life is a true mess if we focus only on this side of our life's frame. What we need to remember is that the knots and swirls of twisted strings that seem to make very little sense are the foundation and structure of the beautiful piece of art we are becoming. We need only to look at the other side.

This beautiful, tangled mess we weave in our work, our relationships, our dreams and our failures are stitching a perfect piece of art in each of us. Welcome the new tangles and knots when they appear. Enjoy them and learn from them for it is the masterpiece of our future selves that we weave.

Flying With Chainsaws
By Mad Chad Taylor

As an entertainer in the college market, I have traveled to many schools to perform my chainsaw juggling. For years, I had checked all of my "supplies" across the country when I was flying until that day. I will never forget an experience that I had shortly after 9/11/01. It was my first time flying post-9/11 and when I reached the front of the baggage check-in line I was informed that it was illegal to check chainsaws on the plane. I had been flying with them for nearly 6 years by this time and no one had ever informed me that it was illegal, but at this point they had called over the airport police and made it clear to me that I could face 6 months in jail and a $250,000 fine for attempting to transport a combustion engine on a commercial airliner.

As I called the programmer at the college that I was attempting to fly to in order to inform him of my predicament, I had a sinking feeling because I had already been forced to cancel several shows due to the incidents of 9/11 and was not looking forward to canceling another one. Well, he was so accommodating, inviting me to still come and do the show without chainsaws. I accepted, made arrangements for a friend to come pick up the saws, checked the rest of my props on the plane and boarded the flight.

Well, that is not the end of the story because when I got to the other end of my flight only one of my prop trunks was there at the baggage carousel. An agent for the airline quickly tracked the other trunk and discovered that the earliest it would make it in would be the next morning. Again, I was forced to call the programmer with bad news and again he was so helpful. He asked me to list all of the props I was missing and he'd see if he could borrow any of the items from around the campus. Again, I was so relieved that we wouldn't have to cancel the show and render my day of traveling useless and miss out on another much needed post-9/11 paycheck, but I couldn't imagine that he would find many of the props that I needed sitting around the campus.

I arrived at the school and this programmer had found a juggler on campus and borrowed almost everything on my list, but I still had no chainsaws and was afraid that the crowd would be so let down by that that they'd boo me off stage. This great programmer introduced me to the audience by explaining what had happened with the chainsaws and really got everybody to understand my problem with a comment about things being changed so much by 9/11 and how we all have to get used to the changes, etc. The crowd was great, and we had a really fun show. It was all due to that programmer going the extra mile for me, and more importantly for his students. At that point everybody needed a good laugh and a fun night to forget about the horrible tragedy of 9/11 and start healing, but if that programmer had thought like I did ("people don't wanna see the chainsaw juggler without his chainsaws") that crowd would have missed out on a fun show that night.

Never forget that a show is about the audience bonding with each other. It would seem that they are bonding with the performer onstage, but in fact they are bonding with each member of the audience. By laughing and applauding or booing and hissing they are agreeing with the rest of the audience: "yes we like this or no we don't like this" and all the while bonding and building a sense of community. Or if it's an emotional experience, like a sad movie, they feel like they have gone through that emotional experience with each other and it brings them close together. So program with that in mind. The more that the audience can interact with the entertainer or the show, or be emotionally moved, the more they interact with each other and create a bond.

Editor's Note: For more information on Mad Chad Taylor, please visit www.madchadtaylor.com.

YOUR LIFE IS TOO SHORT TO DO THE THINGS YOU SUCK AT.™

-ANTHONY J. D'ANGELO

A Dime With Nickels
By Edmund T. Cabellon, M.S.

During the summer of 1996, I worked for a company called Vector Marketing, as an opportunity to apply my Communication and Marketing majors into a work environment. My job was to sell knives, kitchen cutlery to be exact. Many people thought I was crazy to be working for a direct sales company, having to practice my sales pitch to family and friends before getting sales leads from the company to actually sell the product.

Like most things I was involved in during that time in my life (R.A., Campus Ministry activities, Student Government, etc), I put my all into this summer job and applied what I had learned from my activities to try and do a good job. As a first-born, first-generation Filipino-American male, I was taught at an early age that I had to work harder and smarter than everyone around me, if I were to succeed in America. My parents came over from the Philippines to give my brother, sister and me the best life possible, and my father's hard work and sacrifice were great examples for us. I have always been in the minority as long as I can remember (Pacific-Islander, Vertically-Challenged, etc.), so I just always tried to work smarter than everyone else. I was always focused on three things: Family/Friends, Working Smart, and Excellent Hospitality.

Perhaps that is why I sold $25,000 worth of product that summer, and achieved the highest level of salesperson, Field Sales Manager. At the final New England Division meeting in August, my Division Manager, Libby Ricci, who was my mentor at the time, had the opportunity to recognize my accomplishment. He talked about my summer with Vector and my attention to staff, work ethic, and the way I treated people...all great things. Before he invited me up to accept my award for reaching $25,000 in sales, he described me with this phrase:

"Ed is like a dime thrown in with a bunch of nickels...half the size, but worth twice as much."

I lost it...no one had ever thought to describe me in this fashion and it inspired and humbled me. I think of this description anytime I'm feeling down or uninspired. For anyone reading this that is underrepresented, or vertically challenged, or feeling like your half the size...remember this description, because I'm sure it's true of you too.

Fail BIG!
By Duane Brown

I have realized that much of my life is nothing more than the sum total of my fears. I have, in fact, been shaped by a long history of chickening out. Dreams I have had, desires I've fantasized about, goals I've been curious to meet, so many of them have never come to be a reality for me. Here's a ridiculous example: in college I always thought it would be really fun to be a camp counselor, and I would've been good at it too. I had the opportunity one summer and I didn't take my chance. Why? Because I was afraid of not making enough money. So I worked hard in the chemical plant my father worked in all summer. I went back to college that Fall with little more than when I left. I can tell you, there are countless more examples in my life where a little bit of fear has gone a long way to keeping me from enjoying many of the small dreams I've had.

So why do I delight you with these tales of self-deprecating and fear? I'm so glad you asked! And I assume you are asking, because in reality I'm writing this far in advance of you, dear reader, actually laying eyes on these words. So yes, good question indeed! I have often heard people say that what they want out of life is…want to take a guess? That's right…happiness. People want to be happy. I read somewhere that happiness could really be defined as "excitement". People describe happy times as when they are excited and enthused about life and the situations they are in. While we're being honest about things, let's face it: excitement usually involves some sense of risk. Risk is thrilling by nature. So if we're following this logic, in order to happy we have to take some risks!

Sometimes risk equals failure. GREAT! I'd like to personally add that if there's a chance of failure, fail BIG! Fail HUGE! Fail ENORMOUSLY! Sure, there might be some immediate negative consequences: your boss is mad at you, or people might consider you (gasp!) unsuccessful, or even the worst failure scenario, that person you just asked out laughs at you, screams "No Way!" while throwing a drink in your face and storms out of the club. But, oh, the lessons learned! Oh, the experience gained! Oh, the stories you can tell! We have to be realistic about risks in life. Truly, what's the worst that can happen by taking a risk? You fail at something and learn some tremendous lessons from the experience. What do you have to gain? Everything! A chance at unparallel success, satisfaction for following your ideas, perhaps a swanky new swagger knowing you are the one with the…um…"guts" to try something new and innovative.

Risk-taking is rarely included in the leadership skills set. But I want to encourage you to put aside your fears about life (most of which are bogus anyway), start practicing risk-taking. It will take your places in life you would never have dreamed of and earn you the respect of those around you. Seriously, what do you have to lose? Register for that wacky art class you've curiously wondered about, take that trip this summer, and ask her/him out! By the way, it is true that the hottest people are usually the ones who rarely get dates. Why? People are too afraid to ask them out! So take a risk…you might be the only person to ask them out in a long time! The odds are in your favor!

Don't let your life become the sum total of your fears. It is ordinary to be afraid of things. It is extraordinary to take the risk and do it anyway. I regret letting fears take away so much for so long in my life, but risk-taking is a skill I am working on more and more and I have to tell you that it's incredibly rewarding. Even my biggest failures from taking risks have been the most rewarding experiences simply from the incredible lessons learned. You have very little to lose and everything to gain! So as you get ready to jump, remember that you have friends and experience to serve as your parachute. When the door to your future opens at 30,000 feet, it's one hell of a view!

Putting The Big Rocks In First
By Anthony J. D'Angelo

At a recent Collegiate EmPowerment Conference I had the opportunity to watch one of our coaches, Joe Urbanski, facilitate an insightful demonstration with a group of students from Hudson Valley Community College. Joe was facilitating our seminar call *Time & Money: Because You Have None.* The exercise is based on a concept which we first learned from Dr. Stephen Covey in his book, *First Things First.* Joe did an amazing job bringing this exercise to life for the students. Here's what he did:

In the middle of the seminar Joe pulled out a wide-mouth jar and placed it on the table, beside some fist-sized rocks.

After filling the jar to the top with rocks he asked, "Is the jar full?"

Students could see that no more rocks would fit, so they replied, "Yes!"

"Not so fast," he cautioned. He then got some gravel from under the table and added it to the jar, filling the spaces between the rocks. Again, he asked, "Is the jar full?"

This time the doubtful students replied "Probably not."

Then Joe reached a bucket of sand below the table, and dumped it on the jar, filling the spaces between the rocks and the gravel. Once again he asked "Is the jar full?"

"No!" the students shouted.

Finally, Joe grabbed a pitcher of water and filled the jar completely, asking to the students what they could learn from that exercise.

One student leader answered, "If you work at it, you can always fit more into your life."

"No," said Joe. "The point is, if you don't put the big rocks in first...would you ever have gotten any of them in the first place?"

This little story can be applied to all aspects of your life, including event planning. Campus events are composed of many activities, like promoting your event, participating in meetings, creating quality programs, networking with other students, exchanging emails and so on.

The question then becomes: out of all these activities, what are the big rocks? More importantly, are you making sure that they are going first into the jar?

A Not So Random Act of Kindness
By Will Keim, Ph.D.

I have seen many astounding acts of kindness during my twenty years of speaking to over two million college students on more than one thousand college campuses.

Students pitching in to collect money to send a student to see his mother who was dying of cancer. A blood drive to aid automobile victims near campus. Fraternity men who go once a year to a retirement home near their chapter to dance with the older ladies the day before Valentine's Day.

Who could doubt the generosity and goodness of college students! Despite media reports to the contrary, college students care deeply about others and the world in which they live.

But one event, though small in national stature or international importance, touched my heart. At Bethany College in West Virginia, I was speaking at a dinner for student leaders, with my five-year-old son, J. J., sitting next to me. After twelve years on the road, I now take one of my children—Christa, Samantha, J.J. or Hannah—with me on every trip. I have just gotten tired of being away from them.

We were eating dinner, when my son made a strange reptile-like sound and deposited his dinner on the table at what could have been culled, up to that point, a semi-formal event. It is hard in life to always think of the other person when you are dealing with your own agenda and persona embarrassment. In this case, however, I was able to "get over myself" and realize that the little guy was in trouble. We caught the subsequent "blasts" in a bucket quickly provided by one of the student and actually finished the meal---though those with a view of my son's problem passed on dessert!

The big question I then encountered was what to do with his clothes. Being a guy, I reached the conclusion they would be thrown away, justified by the reality that we were traveling and leaving for Cincinnati that night. Suddenly I heard a voice that I now realize belonged to an angel, or perhaps a saint, standing next to me.

She said, "Give me his clothes, and I will wash them during your speech." She was a student at the dinner, she seemed sincere, and I immediately began to question her sanity. Who takes someone else's very dirty clothes and washes them, willingly? We all know it is bad enough doing your own clothes or those of someone you know and love.

"You don't have to do that. I couldn't ask that of you," I said.

"You did not ask," she stated. "And that Tigger sweatshirt is his favorite," she said.

"How do you know that?" I asked.

"Tigger is my favorite too," she replied, "and he and I talked about it during dinner."

I realized then that I had been wrapped up in myself and missed their entire conversation. I knew, too, that I was dealing with an extraordinary young woman who wanted to reach out to someone in need, even though she had never met us before. As she left with the clothes in a trash bag, I turned to her advisor and said, "She is really something! What year is she?" He said, "A freshman, and what you have seen is a regular occurrence with her."

When something silly happens on a campus now, or even a bad thing takes place, I think of that young woman, armed with J.J.'s clothes in a bag, heading for her residence hall. She gives me hope because I know there are others like her. Students who are good and kind—persons who will be in charge of the world my children will grow up in. That night I was supposed to be the "teacher"... but in reality, she was my teacher, and I was her humble student.

That is the beauty of being a good educator. If you are open to the possibilities, there is a good chance that we will exchange roles at times and grow together. As Dean Robert Schaffer of Indiana University once said, "I have to believe that the student's life will be better because we have met rather than if we had not, because I know how much richer my life has become because of my students."

One fall night in Bethany, West Virginia, my life became richer, my purpose empowered, my spirit lifted because of a not-so-random act of kindness by a wonderful college freshman.

Editor's Note: For more information on Will Keim, please visit
www.willkeim.com

There Are Professors and Then There Are Educators
By Anthony J. D'Angelo

When I asked my Biology Professor,
"What Do You Teach?" He said, "Biology."
When I asked my Director of Student Activities,
"What Do You Teach?" She said, "Students."

When I asked my Statistics Professor,
"What Do You Teach?" She said, "Statistics."
When I asked my Director of Greek Life,
"What Do You Teach?" He said, "Students."

When I asked my Literature Professor,
"What Do You Teach?" He said, "Literature."
When I asked my Director of Residence Life,
"What Do You Teach?" She said, "Students."

As I grew older and wiser I realized that I got my degree thanks to
my professors, but I received my education thanks to my student
affairs professionals.

The message to you is simple:
Get To Know Your Student Affairs Professionals.

Even though they are not professors, they are some of the most
powerful educators on your campus. They will help you take your
higher education deeper.

Someone Once Asked
By Sabrina E. Ruch

Someone once asked why I do this.
"Is it because you get paid?"
I'm shocked. No, I'm not paid.
If they were paying me, I wouldn't owe tuition.

> *"Well then why do you do it? Were you recruited?*
No, I was not drafted! I enlisted.

I do it because...
>Well, I do it because...

I do it because I love it.
>*"Oh, so you love how it looks on your résumé?"*

No, I love it because...

...Because I've cleaned blueberry pie off the floor more than once.

...Because I've counted thousands of poker chips into plastic sandwich bags.

...Because I've spent hours painting Christmas ornaments when I should have been studying.

...Because I've spent countless nights calling BINGO numbers hoping for once that the room is silent when I call O-69 and knowing that it will never be.

Inspiration for Student Programmers

…Because I love to hear people, who can't sing, forget the words to their so-called "favorite" songs.

…Because I couldn't have done anything better with these past four years.

I challenge you. Follow your heart.

Find out where your passion lies and don't let anyone take that from you.

Don't do it for the money.

Don't worry about what will look best on your résumé.

Take pride in what you do.

Clean the blueberry pie off the floor and smile.

What Do You Want: Diversity or a Free Lunch?
By Joe Onorio

Diversity. As a programmer at a University it's the one buzz word you hear all the time, right? If we hear it all the time, why do some of us only seem to care about it for a month at a time? How often are you inclined to bring in a Black comedian in February? A female musician in March? Well… can't a woman play music in February or a black comedian be funny in March? And really… is a comic, who happens to be black, really the way we should be teaching our students and peers how to celebrate a "history" month?

One experience that I'll never forget as a professional happened pretty quickly after starting a new job at a college in a large, metropolitan area. In a city filled with diversity, I thought it safe to assume that the idea of educating our students (and as I later discovered, my colleagues) about all kinds of diversity at all times was a safe path to travel. Boy, did I miss the mark big time!

March 1st: the day I (apparently) officially erased Black History Month. Yup, I single handedly cancelled the entire month of February! I arrived at work that morning and was greeted by a few emails and a couple of voicemails from students asking me "what happened to Black History Month?" I was completely beside myself – I couldn't begin to understand what they were asking. Naturally, I was really concerned that these students were upset so I met with them as soon as possible. I, too, wanted to know how Black History Month disappeared. It turns out that my predecessor had planned an event each year celebrating Black

History in February: food in the main hallway of the building.
Food. Fried Chicken, macaroni and cheese, biscuits. I asked the
students what else was done in recognition of Black History month
in the past. The answer: nothing. While I was a bit shocked by
the response, I could not ignore the fact that these students sitting
in front of me were still upset that I erased Black History Month
from their school. I had made a huge mistake…these students
didn't know me yet. They didn't know my philosophies on
programming. All they knew was that I neglected the one tradition
for the month of February that they'd known.

I took some time to explain my position to the students: I don't
believe that education about different cultures and races should
be limited to one month. I also don't believe, and hoped that they
felt the same way, that simply passing out free food is the way
to honor thousands of years of history. While still feeling a little
slighted that they missed out on a free lunch the month prior, they
did understand where I was coming from. We went through the
programming calendar for that quarter and pointed out the many
programs and events that celebrated the diverse differences in our
world and within our college community: lectures, films, museum
and gallery visits, musical performances, and yes – even a
comedian.

Granted, not all of those things happened in the month of February,
but it was important for me to know that these students left
understanding that these things shouldn't only happen in the month
of February. What I really wanted is for these same students to
come to me in April and complain if there was nothing included
in that month's events calendar to teach them or expose them to a
different culture. I wanted them to realize that it was perpetuating
the narrow-mindedness in society when no one speaks up that

everyone's difference aren't celebrated every day simply because there is a notion on their calendar that says it's not the appropriate month to do so.

Feeling better that those students left with a greater understanding of educating through programming (and not relying on food to represent a race/culture), I left my desk to pick up lunch. I was stopped on my way by two African American women who were full time staff members at the college. Instead of the normal "hello" and "how are you doing" I was used to hearing I was greeted with the question, "What happened to Black History Month?" I was definitely less patient with these two women then I had been with the group of students earlier. Perhaps I expected a greater understanding from my colleagues? Perhaps I was just really hungry and needed lunch? I listed every event we'd had that in any way, shape, or form celebrated diversity and asked if they attended (the answer, of course: no)... I asked exactly what they felt was missing. Their answer: the food.

This taught me so many things... most importantly that we as programmers need to teach those around us that we should not settle for celebrations that perpetuate stereotypes as a method of "educating". I asked these women if they could see any reason they should be offended if the college's one tribute to the thousands of years of fascinating history and culture of African Americans boiled down to passing out free fried chicken in the school's main hallway. What if the following month for Women's History Month I had planned on boiling down every woman's contribution to the world by passing out free slices of cake in honor of Betty Crocker? It was clear from the look of their face that they realized what had happened... Black History Month wasn't what they missed. They missed a free lunch. They missed the stereotypes that had been perpetuated in years past as the way their histories should be honored. My hopes are that after March 1st, those students and staff members begin getting angered whenever Blacks are ignored in months other than the shortest of the year...or when Women aren't honored outside of the month of March...or when people simply start buying their own lunch.

A Promise From A Friend
By Anthony J. D'Angelo

I Believe...
I believe success is the freedom to be yourself.
I believe nobody is wrong they are only different.
I believe your circumstances don't define you,
rather they reveal you.
I believe without a sense of caring,
there can be no sense of community.
I believe our minds are like parachutes.
They only work if they are open.
I believe we only live life once,
but if we live it right, one time is all we'll need.
I believe we must first get along with ourselves
before we can get along with others.

I Will...
I will seek to understand you.
I will label bottles, not people.
I will grow antennas, not horns.
I will see the diversity of our commonality.
I will see the commonality of our diversity.
I will get to know who you are rather than what you are.
I will transcend political correctness
and strive for human righteousness.

I Challenge You...
I challenge you to honor who you are.
I challenge you to enjoy your life rather than endure it.
I challenge you to create the status quo rather than accept it.
I challenge you to live in your imagination
more than your memory.
I challenge you to live your life as a revolution
and not just a process of evolution.
I challenge you to ignore other people's ignorance
so that you may discover your own wisdom.

I Promise You...
I promise to do my part.
I promise to stand beside you.
I promise to interrupt the world
when its thinking becomes ignorant.
I promise to believe in you,
even when you have lost faith in yourself.

I am here for you.

Our Hidden Path
By Setheriane Adams

Day of Silence.
Showing the silence brought about by the deaths of others.
Showing that we care.
Making a statement.
But then the event ended.

Our group was falling apart.
Our group was unraveling.
Before our very eyes.
People forgetting.
People leaving.
People not caring.
It started out wonderfully.
Then all the enthusiasm wore off.
Without a cause the passion wasn't there.

Nothing to do to bring us together.
Except for the Day of Silence.
So why not try it again?
Why wait again until next year?

We decided to take action.
Three days to put it together.
Announcements.
Flyers.
Handouts.
Black arm bands to symbolize your involvement.

Hoping people will help out.
Hoping it will fly.

Three days tick away.
It's the big day.
Walking through the halls.
Looking at the others wearing the arm band.

A tiny club with only five members.
Begins to multiply by infinity.
That's the number of supports we saw.
Everywhere you turned another black arm band.

We run out of arm bands.
Kid's staple and tape black paper around their arms.
Then end of the day comes.
We are proud.
We finally touched them.
We finally made an impact.
We found our purpose.
We found our hidden path.

The Day of Silence is an annual event held to bring attention to anti-LGBT bullying, harassment and discrimination in schools. Students and teachers nationwide will observe the day in silence to echo the silence that LGBT and ally students face every day. The Day of Silence is one of the largest student-led actions in the country.

The Day Of Silence Takes Place In The Spring Semester Each Year And Makes for A Great Campus Programming Event. To learn more about future dates: www.DayofSilence.org

2 + 2 = 30
By Edmund T. Cabellon, M.S.

I've always loved math. The logic of it, the memorization of tables, etc. always got me excited. I was always good at it throughout grade school, high school, college, and even on the SAT's! So when I was presented with this equation by one of my classmates in graduate school, it sent me into quite a tizzy!

As part of my "Higher Education Programming" class, we were split into groups to make create a college program or service. During one of the presentations, one of my classmates, Jonah, issued this question to our class: Can 2 + 2 = 30? Of course, being the math aficionado that I was, I immediately raised my hand and said, "NO!" Jonah, with a smile on his face, said back, "Why not?" Becoming increasingly impatient, I responded, "Because it's basic Math, 2 + 2 = 4!"

Jonah then taught me one of my greatest lessons I ever learned in graduate school. He said to our class that our whole life, we had been programmed in our elementary and high school educations. From when we were in second grade we were taught that 2 + 2 = 4 and 4 + 4 = 8, etc. We could probably even recite those tables in our sleep and remember the different ways we learned how to count and do quick math. However, while this was part of the education, it wasn't the entire thing. The other half of our education falls as our responsibility. We need to more than simply "auto respond" to questions we believe we know the answer to.

Jonah then wrote on the board: $2 + 2 = 30$

And then said, "this equation is TRUE. If…" While writing on the board: 2 Dimes + 2 Nickels = 30 Cents

"No one asked me, 2 of WHAT Jonah?"

This one equation taught me one of the greatest lessons I learned in graduate school. We all cannot become complacent in what we know, but what MORE can we know? Instead of saying that a program or advertising technique can't work, I say, HOW can this program or advertising technique work?

I learned a new way of math that day, that has helped me helped many students as a Program Advisor and helped me constantly challenge the way I think.

$2 + 2$ can equal 30 if we simply ask the right questions.

Leadership...Take The First Step!
By Jessica Manjack

Have you ever worked with a group, either as a leader or a member, and wondered why you found some people more difficult to work with than others? It's not likely that they are actually difficult people. It's not even that you are a difficult person to work with. Rather, the difficulty can be attributed to the fact that people have different personality types and leadership styles. The more we all understand these types and styles, the better we can work together.

Leadership is a popular topic in today's society, especially when leaders fail from a legal or moral perspective. It brings to mind a question; "What kind of leader am I?" The role can be demonstrated in many situations ranging from large corporations to neighborhood associations and in my area: student affairs. The kind of leadership that each of us exhibits will depend on several factors: what the circumstance calls for, what strengths we bring to the role, and how we define leadership. My personal definition of leadership is simple: a leader knows what should be done, and a manager knows how it should be done.

Through my experiences within the area of student affairs, especially student activities, I have been able to perfect my skills as a leader and challenge my capabilities as a key contributor to any organization in which I become involved as well as the type of job I pursue in the future. I have developed some personal leadership qualities that I feel make me a good leader. My first belief is that a leader should not be afraid to change things.

Secondly, one must lead by example. Do the things you want your followers to do.

Leadership also has applications that extend beyond the university setting. It is extremely valuable in all types of career fields, and the university provides an opportunity for students to gain a broad-based leadership experience. The value of this cannot be measured. Therefore, students should make the most of their leadership experience and strive to be effective student leaders.

Becoming an active member in clubs and organizations on campus is a great way to meet new people and participate in something that you enjoy. I have been able to learn so much from my experiences of involvement on campus as an undergraduate student, graduate student and as a professional. I think everyone should be able to have that same opportunity. Even if you are hesitant about it at first, just take that first step of joining a club or organization that interests you and give it your all!

You Never Know
By Bethany Lombard

In August 1997, I began a job at a two-year institution on the East Coast. After spending several years in Residence Life and Judicial Affairs, I was making the leap to Student Activities. How challenging could it really be? Well I was about to find out.

When I arrived on campus to begin my job, the first thing I needed to do was meet the Executive Board of the Campus Activities Board and see what programs they had planned for the fall. I set up a meeting with the Board and quickly discovered that it was only two people. Even though Student Activities was new to me, I knew this was not good. At the meeting we discussed what they had planned for the semester, and you guessed it, two programs. The X-Rated Hypnotist for Welcome Weekend and a semi-formal in December. I thought to myself, that's a lot of space in between. But I was always taught to never let them see you sweat. As a group of three we talked about performers that they had seen at NACA Regional COnference and I went to work booking away. For the most part it worked out – I even was able to manage to get the one performer they wanted most, Mike Super. For a rookie, I certainly felt like I could do this and we did make it happen as a group. Programming was great and it set us up for a great second semester. Check.

Next step, get a programming board. At a two-year institution, that meant we were pretty much looking at the first-year students. After all, the second year students had other commitments other than the two executive board members that we already had. We did the typical Involvement Fair on a Tuesday, gave out little trinkets and candy and got students to put their names on a list, but that doesn't translate to a programming board. Our first meeting was that Thursday. Would all 30 of those students that "signed up" show up. You guessed it…NO. In fact only ten of them did but there was one student that showed up that wasn't on the list – Gina.

Our agenda, started with introductions and why you came to the meeting that night. When we got to Gina and she was asked why she came, her answer was "because it was the only thing on the campus calendar for tonight." Well that certainly said a lot. Next my two executive board members talked about what we were planning, what each member of the group would do at events, and that we were still looking for a Secretary for the executive board, the President then asks if anyone is interested. Silence until Gina asks, "What do you have to do?" We explain that its taking minutes, giving a report at meetings. She nods as if she understands. There was something about Gina that just struck me. So I jumped in and outright asked her, "Are you interested?' She says, "sure." Very quickly, I motion to the President to get this approved by everyone…it will be there first group decision. The students are more likely to feel invested if they know they already have a voice. Gina became the secretary. The students in that room the night of the meeting helped us set up for our next event, and eight of them stuck it out for the year including Gina.

Gina not only was secretary, she ended up to be President in her second year. She attended an NACA National Convention in Indianapolis, two Regional Conferences, and even became one of my RAs. She went onto graduate from a four year institution and has a great job managing people at a fitness center. We have kept in touch sporadically, but I always knew that what she learned from her leadership roles and experiences would take her to great places.

Fast forward to April 2007. I actually run into her Mom in the mall. She tells me Gina is getting married in September. How exciting!! After exchanging numbers, we depart but I am so glad to reconnect. I end up going to her bridal shower and wedding! Her thank you note from the bridal shower read, "You are a big part of how I survived college and became a polished business professional. I was very fortunate that you saw something special in me and pulled me through." As much as I taught Gina, she taught me more than she will ever know.

As a student programmer, always remember that each person that walks into your meeting or program is there for a reason. You may not know it at that time but you may change their life or they may change yours. You never know.

The Joys of Being a Student Programmer
By Holly Nonnemacher

J – Job experience – This is real world experience that you are gaining and will definitely help you make the transition from classroom to boardroom. Only a select few college graduates can talk about the casino night that they organized for 1000 of their classmates or the budget of $50,000 that they oversaw each semester.

O – Optimism – You are learning to see the positive in every situation. The opening band didn't show up for your concert, instead of stressing, you look at this as a great opportunity for your advisor to test out their comedy routine (I don't recommend this).

Y – Youthfulness – Where else can you find adults doing things like putting on sumo suits and wrestling or sitting in a giant inflatable chair to have their picture taken? As a student programmer you have the opportunity to relive some of the most fun and entertaining events from your childhood. These not only allow you to take a trip down memory lane, they also allow you to remain young at heart. And if you ever doubt this, just ask your advisor about the youthfulness they feel everyday!

S – Sanity – You are learning how to deal with stressful situations and keep your sanity – this is an amazing lesson that many don't learn until their sanity has already been lost. Just ask your advisor and I'm sure they have stories about those who didn't learn this lesson.

Inspired By Inspiration
By Erin Roberts

I was one of the lucky people that thought I knew exactly what I wanted to do when I came to college. I had made the decision to transfer from a highly esteemed nursing program at a well reputed private college to the Early Childhood Education program at Bridgewater State College. I "knew" that I wanted to be a preschool teacher and work with children as a career. I wanted to be someone who had a hand in helping shape the lives of people. I defined myself as a teacher and was excited to start myself on the path that I should have been on all along.

Upon transferring, I made the decision to become involved in Program Committee (PC) so that I could help plan events and activities for the campus. I was very interested in being involved in an organization on campus and thought that PC would be a great way to get that involvement. In the fall of 2005, I attended the NACA Northeast conference with PC and was amazed with how much it had to offer. I loved everything about the conference and was excited for the chance to get more involved both with NACA and with PC at my campus.

In 2006, I went to the NACA Northeast conference that ultimately changed my life. As a returning delegate, I felt like I had more of an opportunity to explore the content of what the marketplaces, showcases, and educational sessions had to offer, rather than just the face value of what I could physically obtain from these events. I had attended a few different educational sessions with the Collegiate EmPowerment group and was excited to check out their booth at the Marketplace. At the booth, I talked to Joe Urbanski about how much I appreciated the sessions that I had attended, and I picked up a copy of *Inspiration for Student Leaders*. I never knew that just one book could help change my life, but it did.

I wasted no time reading the book. At the following showcase session I read the entire book front to back. I read all of the personal stories about how people made their decision to go into the field of Higher Education and was so inspired to make a difference in someone's life. I was incredibly inspired by each and every story, anecdote, tale, and quote in that book that I couldn't put it down. I thought to myself, "I want to do that. I want to help someone become a better person. I want to affect someone the same way that the authors in this book and the professionals that I work with have affected me." I was excited at the chance that pursuing a career in Student Affairs was a possibility for me, but I was scared to make another major change in my life.

After returning to campus, I had a conversation with Matt Miller, the advisor of Program Committee, about what I had been thinking about for a while. I sat in his office and told him about how I wanted to go into Student Affairs and how excited I would be to work with college students. I explained how scared I was to pursue such a career though. Teaching was the one thing in my life that I had always been certain of. It was the one thing that I always knew I wanted to do, the thing that brought me to this school, the thing that got me to be a student leader. How could I just drop something like that for something I was so uncertain of?

Matt's words were simple: "Isn't what I do teaching?" That's when I realized that working in the field of Higher Education is just like teaching, and a career in Student Affairs would actually have more of an impact on people than my career as a preschool teacher. As a Student Affairs professional, you have the opportunity to work with amazing student leaders' day in and day out. You get to help these students in one of the most impressionable and memorable times of their lives. The students that you work with aren't your typical run-of-the-mill college students, but rather outstanding and empowered students who are making the most out of their college experience and that are taking their Higher Education deeper. As someone working in Student Affairs, you get the privilege and the opportunity to help people figure out who they are and what they want to do with their lives, much like my advisor did for me.

So what did I do? I got more involved and am taking advantage of every opportunity that I have to be involved on this campus. I ran for and was elected Vice-President of Program Committee. I ran for and was elected President of my Senior class. I serve as a senator on the Student Government Association. I am actively involved in the planning and organization of all of the senior events for the school year. I am an Orientation Leader. I serve on the Student Affairs Committee as a student representative. I am a Class Marshall. I am involved in a peer outreach group. I am a founder and an advisor of the Student Weekend Activities Team. I am actively involved with various volunteer opportunities through NACA. I am a Student Leader.

Being a Student Leader is a tough job and no one knows how hard it is to balance being a student with being a leader better than I do. But being a Student Leader really is about figuring out what you want to get from the experience. I became a student leader to simply get more involved as a student. However, the experiences that I heard about through the *Inspiration for Student Leaders* book helped me see how to get the most out of my leadership experience. To this day, almost two years later, whenever I am having a bad day or I am questioning why I am doing everything that I am involved in, I pick up the book and open to a random story and I remember. I hope that everyone can find something as constant and inspiring in their lives as this book is to me.

I am excited to go forward to pursue a career in the field of Higher Education and Student Development. I can only hope that one day I will have helped and inspired someone even half as much as my advisor Matt, the Inspiration series, and Joe and the Collegiate EmPowerment crew has helped and inspired me. If I can ever say that I have done so, then I will be happy and know that I made the right decision.

Pizza and A Dream Career
By Michael Dean Ester

Few young people go off to college and join the activities board thinking it's a career move. I know I didn't. I walked in looking for pizza and walked out with a dream career.

I was probably about eight years old when I told my parents, "I want to be a comedian when I grow up."

They patted my head and gave me the kind of all-purpose encouragement that moms and dads heap upon their young dreamers. "You can do anything you want," they said. It was like I had just told them I wanted to be an astronaut.

I went off to college with the kind of all-purpose enthusiasm that comes from having no plan in particular, buoyed by the belief that professors would be handing out dreams as a part of everyone's freshman seminar. For a hundred thousand dollars per degree, I decided, the school ought to be handing out dream careers, too. I was wrong, of course. College allows you to zero in on a career once you've got a dream in mind, but there's no course offered to light a fire in your imagination and tell you what to dream in the first place: comedian, astronaut, whatever.

As I worked my way through randomly selected classes, one campus extra-curricular called to me: Theatre. I thought the decision to choose dramatic arts as a major would mark the day my life changed forever. I would focus like a laser beam on my future as a performer. Unfortunately, the only noticeable change was in

the way I started switching the last two letters of the word theater.
The more acting roles I played, the less excitement I felt about
taking the stage to recite other people's words. My career plan
seemed to run parallel to my dream without ever touching it.

Salvation came in the form of an unlikely sign on the bulletin
board: "Help CAB pick next year's comedians. Free pizza." Pizza
and comedy, I thought. Aside from God and Steeler football, I
couldn't think of anything I loved more.

The special CAB meeting happened the next day. I recall stuffing
my face with pepperoni-double-cheese slices while the comedy
chair juggled VHS tapes. We must have watched a dozen different
comics. The more acts I saw, however, the more I felt a churning
in my stomach. At first, I thought it was the pizza. I stopped eating.
I stopped laughing at the comedians. My reaction changed from
amusement to appreciation to something that felt like ... envy. It
occurred to me that I was watching other people live my dream. It
was a huge revelation.

I took over as comedy chair the following year. I welcomed
each visiting performer with a sense of wonder. None of these
comedians were celebrities. I only recognized them from
their video tapes. However, I respected them as hard-working
entertainers who toured the country one campus at a time. They
were smart, hip, opinionated professionals who knew how to relate
to college students. They took the stage and talked about life on
their own terms, using their own words, and they got huge laughs.
More than anything, I knew I wanted to be one of them. I had
never known such certainty in my life.

One day during my junior year, I worked up the courage to mention my dream to Tim Settimi, the versatile comedian who had recently been voted NACA Campus Entertainer of the Year. "You can do anything you want," he replied, echoing my parents' sentiment from many years earlier. Tim, however, went a step further. "How bad do you want it?"

"More than anything," I said.

Tim smiled and shook my hand. "If that's really true," he said, "I'll see you up on stage. People work like crazy for something if they really want it in their hearts."

I started working right away. I wrote material and tried the jokes on anyone who would listen. During the summer before my senior year, I stayed with my roommate in the New York City area and took a pair of comedy classes in Manhattan. Back on campus in the fall, I opened for every visiting performer, forcing myself to write a brand new monologue to warm up the crowd for each comedy event. I wrote and re-wrote my stuff, I worked on my delivery, I honed my act.

After graduation, I moved east and took jobs answering phones and cleaning offices while I tramped my way to every open mic night in New York and New Jersey. I picked up occasional weekend work at local comedy clubs. Within three or four years, I had steady work as a club comic on weekends and hosted my own Tuesday night show at a comedy club/coffee house in Red Bank, NJ. I got to know a lot of other comedians. One of them worked on the college market and took me along as an opening act at a few schools. As it turned out, the program boards filled out report cards on me and sent them to NACA. People started paying attention.

Fast forward another year and I had a college agency. My act was ready to be marketed to schools nationwide. It was my turn to be the face on a VHS tape. In 1995, I was selected for my first NACA Conference showcase. It was the Upper Midwest Regional and I remember how strange it felt to be standing on stage performing for activities board members who were wearing the same kind of name tag I had worn at a NACA Conference as a student.

I booked a lot of shows from the conference. The first one took place a few months later at a community college in Iowa. I learned that it was scheduled to be a two-person show. I gasped when I saw the backdrop behind the stage. It said, "Student Activities welcomes Michael Dean Ester and Tim Settimi."

I have always been grateful for my involvement with student activities. It inspired a dream that I have been living for more than twelve years now. My comedy show has evolved in that time. After nearly a thousand campus appearances, it has become a thinly veiled motivational program. I am a comedian on a mission. I want all college graduates to love their careers as much as I love mine. Every time I take the stage on campus, I am there to inspire others by delivering a message about success with every punch line. Here it is:

Successful people don't work harder or work smarter or work longer. The truth is that successful people don't work at all. Successful people love what they do. If you love what you do, you'll never work a day in your life. Isn't that why we go to college in the first place?

Not long ago, I performed my show (aptly titled, "The Reason You're Here!") at Embry Riddle Aeronautical University in

Arizona. I talked to some of the smartest and most career-focused individuals I've ever met. After the show, I had dinner with the activities board, many of whom were already licensed pilots. I told them the story of how my parents patted me on the head when I announced my dream of becoming a comedian as if I had told them I was going to be an astronaut.

"I know what you mean," one student said. "I told my mom I'm going to be an astronaut. She said: What are you ... a comedian?"

Editor's Note: Michael Dean Ester is a past
nominee for Comedian of the Year by NACA.
He is represented by Neon Entertainment 800-993-NEON.

inspire

Permissions & Trademarks

We would like to thank the following contributing authors for their permission to reprint their submissions:

An Advisor's Wish For You © 2007 Christa Sandelier
What I Thought About My Programming Board Advisor During...
© 2007 Anthony J. D'Angelo
What Every College Creed Ought To Be
© 1995 Anthony J. D'Angelo
The Door © 2007 Ana Maria Tosado-Bernier, M.S.
Becoming A Better Me © 2007 Anne Ritchie
For Those Who Doubt © 2007 Holly Nonnemacher
Sacred Work © 2007 Duane Brown
Leadership Is About Purpose, Not Position © 2007 Jack Gottlieb
Endless Opportunities For Networking © 2007 Stephanie Thomas
Follow Your Yellow Brick Road © 2007 Stephanie Russell Holz
Semper Gumby! © 2007 Anthony J. D'Angelo
A Funny Thing Happened On The Way To The Event
© 2007 Gary Teurack
The Coin Of Indecision © 2007 Sean Adams
Find Your Voice, Through The Whisper Of Another
© Jack Gottlieb
Rainbow Flag Number 7 © 2002 Ken Schneck
What It Means To Be A Programmer © 2007 Joe Urbanski
Putting The Big Rocks In First © 2007 Anthony J. D'Angelo
Seven Programming Tips For Events
© 2004 Will Keim, PhD
Does Size Really Matter? © 2007 Jen Bothwell
A New Tradition Starts Somewhere © 2007 Erin Morrell, M.A.
A Beautiful Mess © 2007 Duane Brown
Flying With Chainsaws © 2007 Mad Chad Taylor

Inspiration for Student Programmers

A Dime With Nickels © 2007 Edmund T. Cabellon, M.S.
The Boy Under The Tree
© 1998 David Coleman and Kevin Randall
Someone Once Asked © 2007 Sabrina E. Ruch
The Rock Star Treatment © 2007 Anthony J. D'Angelo
A Promise From A Friend © 2007 Anthony J. D'Angelo
A Not So Random Act Of Kindness © 1999 Will Keim, PhD
2 + 2 = 30 © 2007 Edmund T. Cabellon, M.S.
What Do You Want: Diversity Or A Free Lunch?
© 2007 Joe Onorio
Leadership...Take The First Step © 2007 Jessica Manjack
Our Hidden Path © 2002 Setheriane Adams
Mr. Frigid © 2007 Robert J. Kerr
The Joys Of Being A Student Programmer
© 2007 Holly Nonnemacher
You Never Know © 2007 Bethany Lombard
There Are Professors And Then There Are Educators
© 1998 Anthony J. D'Angelo
Fail BIG! © 2007 Duane Brown
Inspired By Inspiration © 2007 Erin Roberts
Pizza And A Dream Career © 2007 Michael Dean Ester

Collegiate EmPowerment

Helping You Take Higher Education Deeper™

The Collegiate EmPowerment Overview

Collegiate EmPowerment is a nationally recognized educational organization exclusively dedicated to serving highly motivated college students and dedicated professionals within the community of Higher Education with the most interactive, inspiring and informative seminars, products, and services. Since 1995, we have served over 1.5 million college students and 35,000 Higher Education Professionals from over 2,500 colleges across North America.

The Student Seminar Series

Professional Development

Books, Posters, Post Cards, & CDs

Expanded Seminar & Coaching Formats

The Student Seminar Series

Taking A Deeper Look...

ORIENTATION

Get A Life... Outside The Classroom™	Get An Education Not Just A Degree™	How To Maximize Your BUZZ!™

LEADERSHIP

You Can't Lead Others Until You First Lead Yourself	Unleashing The Mindset of A Champion™	Time & Money... Because You Have None

ORGANIZATIONS

Why Most Student Organizations Don't Work™	Passing The Torch™	Cultivating Team Synergy™

GRADUATION

Preventing A Miserable Career Journey™	Get A Life... After College	Taking Higher Education Higher

Collegiate
EmPowerment

Helping You Take Higher Education Deeper™

The Collegiate EmPowerment Approach

Thank you for allowing Collegiate EmPowerment the opportunity to serve you and
your campus community. What follows is an overview of your customized
Collegiate EmPowerment Experience. Each experience has been designed using
The Collegiate EmPowerment Approach. Here's how it works:

INFORMATION
The Collegiate EmPowerment Concepts
In their thirst for knowledge most people are drowning in all the information.
We cut through all the pointless junk and give you only the good stuff!

INSPIRATION
The Collegiate EmPowerment Videos, Music & Interaction
Your mind never forgets what your heart remembers.
Emotion= Energy In Motion. This helps the information stick!

ASSOCIATION
The Collegiate EmPowerment Relationship Process
If we can't relate to you, you can't relate to us.
That's why our services are created by passionate professionals
for passionate students and professionals.
No boring stiff suits behind a podium!

APPLICATION
The Collegiate EmPowerment Tools & Exercises
EmPowerment is taking immediate, massive, focused action.
With immediate application, you create relevant and lasting impact on campus!

All of our seminars are customized around you and the needs
of your unique campus community. You are at the center of
everything we do. Once we understand you and your needs,
we then design your Collegiate EmPowerment Experience
to transform people's lives!

Collegiate EmPowerment
Helping You Take Higher Education Deeper™

The Collegiate EmPowerment Package
Helping You Taking Higher Education Deeper™

The Seminar Experience Design & Delivery Process

1. The Consultation Call:
To Understand Your Needs & How We Can Best Serve You
2. The Commitment Call:
To Finalize Seminar Details (Focus, Date, Time, Budget, Etc.)
3. The Pre-Seminar Interview:
To Co-Create The Seminar Based On Your Needs
4. The Customization Process:
Creating The Best Experience For Your Students
5. The Pre-Seminar Courtesy Call:
To Ensure Confidence In All Logistics
6. The Post-Seminar Assessment:
To Reflect Upon & Build Off Your Success
7. The Quarterly Follow-Up Call:
To Ensure Consistent & Lasting Impact

Value Enhancements Included With Seminar
Creating EmPowering Relationships With You & Your Students
• Optional 20-Minute Question & Answer Session
• Post-Seminar Meal With Student Leaders
• Post-Seminar Assessment Call With Client
• Personalized Contact With Seminar Coach/Facilitator
• Immediate Enrollment In The EmPowerEdge

To learn more about Collegiate EmPowerment:
Contact 877-EDUTAIN (338-8246)
or visit www.Collegiate-EmPowerment.org

......checkout**these
other**gr**eat
book**s

from Collegiate EmPowerment...

SO WHAT about YOU?

you have an insightful & inspiring story about your collegiate experience?

We are looking for stories that exemplify the collegiate life experience. If you are in college- we know you've got a story inside of you to share with others. The purpose of the Inspiration Book Series is to inspire college students by sharing your own story. We are looking for stories, poems, pictures and artwork that touch the heart, open the mind and rekindle the spirit of college students across the country.

Inspiration stories are personal and often filled with emotion. They are real stories by real people for real students. Our stories have heart, but also something extra, that special element that makes us all feel more hopeful, more thankful and more alive. They help us all remember why we got involved in this "thing" in the first place.

Most of all they remind us to take Higher Education Deeper.

We are actively seeking submissions as well as Co Authors for the following future Inspiration Book Projects:

Inspiration for Resident Assistants, Vol. II
Inspiration for Community College Students
Inspiration for International Students
Inspiration for Community Builders
Inspiration for Pre-Med Students
Inspiration for Law Students
Inspiration for MBA Students
Inspiration for University Women
Inspiration for Student Government Members
Inspiration for African American Students
Inspiration for Asian American Students
Inspiration for Latino & Hispanic Students
Inspiration for Student Athletes
Inspiration for College Cheerleaders
Inspiration for Fraternity Men
Inspiration for Sorority Women

For More Information Please Contact:
Collegiate EmPowerment
www.Collegiate-EmPowerment.org
Toll Free: 1.877.EDUTAIN (338.8246)
Email your submission to:
Info@Collegiate-EmPowerment.org

Get A Life... Outside The Classroom®